THE FLIGHT OF THE EAGLE

The Flight of The Eagle

Authentic Report of Talks and Discussions
in London, Amsterdam, Paris,
and Saanen, Switzerland

J. Krishnamurti

Perennial Library
Harper & Row, Publishers
New York, Evanston, San Francisco

Contents

"The eagle in its flight does not leave a mark; the scientist does. Inquiring into this question of freedom, there must be not only scientific observation, but also the flight of the eagle that does not leave a mark."

1. *Freedom*

Thought, pleasure and pain.

For most of us, freedom is an idea and not an actuality. When we talk about freedom, we want to be free outwardly, to do what we like, to travel, to be free to express ourselves in different ways, free to think what we like. The outward expression of freedom seems to be extraordinarily important, especially in countries where there is tyranny, dictatorship; and in those countries where outward freedom is possible one seeks more and more pleasure, more and more possessions.

If we are to inquire deeply into what freedom implies, to be inwardly, completely and totally free—which then expresses itself outwardly in society, in relationship—then we must ask, it seems to me, whether the human mind, heavily conditioned as it is, can ever be free at all. Must it always live and function within the frontiers of its own conditioning, so that there is no possibility of freedom at all? One sees that the mind, verbally understanding that there is no freedom here on this earth, inwardly or outwardly, then begins to invent freedom in another world, a future liberation, heaven and so on.

Put aside all theoretical, ideological, concepts of freedom so that we can inquire whether our minds, yours and mine, can ever be actually free, free from dependence, free from fear, anxiety, and free from the innumerable problems, both the conscious as well as those at the deeper

1

layers of the unconscious. Can there be complete psychological freedom, so that the human mind can come upon something which is not of time, which is not put together by thought, yet which is not an escape from the actual realities of daily existence?

Unless the human mind is inwardly, psychologically, totally free it is not possible to see what is true, to see if there is a reality not invented by fear, not shaped by the society or the culture in which we live, and which is not an escape from the daily monotony, with its boredom, loneliness, despair and anxiety. To find out if there is actually such freedom one must be aware of one's own conditioning, of the problems, of the monotonous shallowness, emptiness, insufficiency of one's daily life, and above all one must be aware of fear. One must be aware of oneself neither introspectively nor analytically, but actually be aware of oneself as one is and see if it is at all possible to be entirely free of all those issues that seem to clog the mind.

To explore, as we are going to do, there must be freedom, not at the end, but right at the beginning. Unless one is free one cannot explore, investigate or examine. To look deeply there needs to be, not only freedom, but the discipline that is necessary to observe; freedom and discipline go together (not that one must be disciplined in order to be free). We are using the word "discipline" not in the accepted, traditional sense, which is to conform, imitate, suppress, follow a set pattern; but rather as the root meaning of that word, which is "to learn." Learning and freedom go together, freedom bringing its own discipline; not a discipline imposed by the mind in order to achieve a certain result. These two things are essential: freedom and the act of learning. One cannot learn about oneself unless one is free, free so that one can observe, not according to any pattern, formula or concept, but actually observe oneself as one is. That observation, that perception, that seeing, brings about its own discipline and learning; in that there is no conformity, imitation,

2

suppression or control whatsoever—and in that there is great beauty.

Our minds are conditioned—that is an obvious fact—conditioned by a particular culture or society, influenced by various impressions, by the strains and stresses of relationships, by economic, climatic, educational factors, by religious conformity and so on. Our minds are trained to accept fear and to escape, if we can, from that fear, never being able to resolve, totally and completely, the whole nature and structure of fear. So our first question is: can the mind, so heavily burdened, resolve completely, not only its conditioning, but also its fears? Because it is fear that makes us accept conditioning.

Do not merely hear a lot of words and ideas—which are really of no value at all—but through the act of listening, observing your own states of mind, both verbally and nonverbally, simply inquire whether the mind can ever be free—not accepting fear, not escaping, not saying, "I must develop courage, resistance," but actually being fully aware of the fear in which one is trapped. Unless one is free from this quality of fear one cannot see very clearly, deeply; and obviously, when there is fear there is no love.

So, can the mind actually ever be free of fear? That seems to me to be—for any person who is at all serious—one of the most primary and essential questions which must be asked and which must be resolved. There are physical fears and psychological fears. The physical fears of pain and the psychological fears as memory of having had pain in the past, and the idea of the repetition of that pain in the future; also, the fears of old age, death, the fears of physical insecurity, the fears of the uncertainty of tomorrow, the fears of not being able to be a great success, not being able to achieve—of not being somebody in this rather ugly world; the fears of destruction, the fears of loneliness, not being able to love or be loved, and so on; the conscious fears as well as the unconscious fears. Can the mind be free, totally, of all this? If the mind says it cannot, then it has made itself incapable, it has distorted

3

itself and is incapable of perception, of understanding; incapable of being completely silent, quiet; it is like a mind in the dark, seeking light and never finding it, and therefore inventing a "light" of words, concepts, theories.

How is a mind which is so heavily burdened with fear, with all its conditioning, ever to be free of it? Or must we accept fear as an inevitable thing of life?—and most of us do accept it, put up with it. What shall we do? How shall I, the human being, you as the human being, be rid of this fear?—not be rid of a particular fear, but of the total fear, the whole nature and structure of fear?

What is fear? (Don't accept, if I may suggest, what the speaker is saying; the speaker has no authority whatsoever, he is not a teacher, he is not a guru; because if he is a teacher then you are the follower and if you are the follower you destroy yourself as well as the teacher.) We are trying to find out what is the truth of this question of fear so completely that the mind is never afraid, therefore free of all dependence on another, inwardly, psychologically. The beauty of freedom is that you do not leave a mark. The eagle in its flight does not leave a mark; the scientist does. Inquiring into this question of freedom there must be, not only the scientific observation, but also the flight of the eagle that does not leave a mark at all; both are required; there must be both the verbal explanation and the nonverbal perception—for the description is never the actuality that is described; the explanation is obviously never the thing that is explained; the word is never the thing.

If all this is very clear then we can proceed; we can find out for ourselves—not through the speaker, not through his words, not through his ideas or thoughts—whether the mind can be completely free from fear.

The first part is not an introduction; if you have not heard it clearly and understood it, you cannot go on to the next.

To inquire there must be freedom to look; there must be freedom from prejudice, from conclusions, concepts,

4

ideals, prejudices, so that you can observe actually for yourself what fear is. *When you observe very closely, intimately, is there fear at all?* That is: you can observe very, very closely, intimately, what fear is only when the "observer" is the "observed." We are going to go into that. So what is fear? How does it come about? The obvious physical fears can be understood, like the physical dangers, to which there is instant response; they are fairly easy to understand; we need not go into them too much. But we are talking about psychological fears; how do these psychological fears arise? What is their origin?—that is the issue. There is the fear of something that happened yesterday; the fear of something that might happen later on today or tomorrow. There is the fear of what we have known, and there is the fear of the unknown, which is tomorrow. One can see for oneself very clearly that fear arises through the structure of thought—through thinking about that which happened yesterday of which one is afraid, or through thinking about the future—right? Thought breeds fear—doesn't it? Please let us be quite sure; do not accept what the speaker is saying; be absolutely sure for yourself, as to whether thought is the origin of fear. Thinking about the pain, the psychological pain that one had some time ago and not wanting it repeated, not wanting to have that thing recalled, thinking about all this breeds fear. Can we go on from there? Unless we see this very clearly we will not be able to go any further. Thought, thinking about an incident, an experience, a state, in which there has been a disturbance, danger, grief or pain, brings about fear. And thought, having established a certain security, psychologically, does not want that security to be disturbed; any disturbance is a danger and therefore there is fear.

Thought is responsible for fear; also, thought is responsible for pleasure. One has had a happy experience; thought thinks about it and wants it perpetuated; when that is not possible there is a resistance, anger, despair and fear. So thought is responsible for fear as well as pleasure—isn't it? This is not a verbal conclusion; this is not a formula for avoiding fear. That is, where there is pleasure there is pain and fear perpetuated by thought; pleasure goes with pain, the two are indivisible, and thought is responsible for both. If there were no tomorrow, no next moment, about which to think in terms of either fear or pleasure, then neither would exist. Shall we go on from there? Is it an actuality, not as an idea, but a thing that you yourself have discovered and which is therefore real, so you can say, "I've found out that thought breeds both pleasure and fear"? You have had sexual enjoyment, pleasure; later you think about it in the imagery, the pictures of thinking, and the very thinking about it gives strength to that pleasure which is now in the imagery of thought, and when that is thwarted there is pain, anxiety, fear, jealousy, annoyance, anger, brutality. And we are not saying that you must not have pleasure.

Bliss is not pleasure; ecstasy is not brought about by thought; it is an entirely different thing. You can come upon bliss or ecstasy only when you understand the nature of thought—which breeds both pleasure and fear.

So the question arises: can one stop thought? If thought breeds fear and pleasure—for where there is pleasure there must be pain, which is fairly obvious—then one asks oneself: can thought come to an end?—which does not mean the ending of the perception of beauty, the enjoyment of beauty. It is like seeing the beauty of a cloud or a tree and enjoying it totally, completely, fully; but when thought seeks to have that same experience tomorrow, that same delight that it had yesterday seeing that cloud, that tree, that flower, the face of that beautiful person, then it invites disappointment, pain, fear and pleasure.

So can thought come to an end? Or is that a wrong question altogether? It is a wrong question because we want to experience an ecstasy, a bliss, which is not pleasure. By ending thought we hope we shall come upon something which is immense, which is not the product of pleasure and fear. What place has thought in life?—not, how is thought to be ended? What is the relationship of thought to action and to inaction? What is the relationship of thought to action where action is necessary? Why, when there is complete enjoyment of beauty, does thought come into existence at all?—for if it did not then it would not be carried over to tomorrow. I want to find out— when there is complete enjoyment of the beauty of a mountain, of a beautiful face, a sheet of water—why thought should come there and give a twist to it and say, "I must have that pleasure again tomorrow." I have to find out what the relationship of thought is in action; and to find out if thought need interfere when there is no need of thought at all. I see a beautiful tree, without a single leaf, against the sky, it is extraordinarily beautiful and that is enough—finished. Why should thought come in and say, "I must have that same delight tomorrow"? And I also see that thought must operate in action. Skill in action is also skill in thought. So, what is the actual relationship between thought and action? As it is, our action is based on concepts, on ideas. I have an idea or concept of what should be done and what is done is approximation to that concept, idea, to that ideal. So there is a division between action and the concept, the ideal, the "should be"; in this division there is conflict. Any division, psychological division, must breed conflict. I am asking myself, "What is the relationship of thought in action?" If there is division between the action and the idea then action is incomplete. Is there an action in which thought sees something instantly and acts immediately so that there is not an idea, an ideology to be acted on separately? Is there an action in which the very seeing is the action—in which the very thinking is the action? I see that thought breeds fear and pleasure; I see that where there is pleasure there is pain and therefore resistance to pain. I see that very clearly; the seeing of it is the immediate action; in the seeing of it is involved thought, logic and thinking very clearly; yet the seeing of it is instantaneous and the action is instantaneous—therefore there is freedom from it.

7

Are we communicating with each other? Go slowly, it is quite difficult. Please do not say, so easily, "yes." If you say "yes," then when you leave the hall, you must be free of fear. Your saying "yes" is merely an assertion that you have understood verbally, intellectually—which is nothing at all. You and I are here this morning investigating the question of fear and when you leave the hall there must be complete freedom from it. That means you are a free human being, a different human being, totally transformed —not tomorrow, but now; you see very clearly that thought breeds fear and pleasure; you see that all our values are based on fear and pleasure—moral, ethical, social, religious, spiritual. If you perceive the truth of it— and to see the truth of it you have to be extraordinarily aware, logically, healthily, sanely observing every movement of thought—then that very perception is total action and therefore when you leave you are completely out of it —otherwise you will say, "How am I to be free of fear, tomorrow?"

Thought must operate in action. When you have to go to your house you must think; or to catch a bus, train, go to the office, thought then operates efficiently, objectively, nonpersonally, nonemotionally; that thought is vital. But when thought carries on that experience that you have had, carries it on through memory into the future, then such action is incomplete, therefore there is a form of resistance and so on.

Then we can go on to the next question. Let us put it this way: what is the origin of thought, and who is the thinker? One can see that thought is the response of knowledge, experience, as accumulated memory, the background from which there is a response of thought to any challenge; if you are asked where you live there is instant response. Memory, experience, knowledge is the background, is that from which thought comes. So thought is never new; thought is always old; thought can never be free, because it is tied to the past and therefore it can never see anything new. When I understand that, very clearly, the mind becomes quiet. Life is a movement, a constant movement in relationship; and thought, trying to capture that movement in terms of the past, as memory, is afraid of life.

Seeing all this, seeing that freedom is necessary to examine—and to examine very clearly there must be the discipline of learning and not of suppression and imitation —seeing how the mind is conditioned by society, by the past, seeing that all thought springing from the brain is old and therefore incapable of understanding anything new, then the mind becomes completely quiet—not controlled, not shaped to be quiet. There is no system or method—it does not matter whether it is Zen from Japan, or a system from India—to make the mind quiet; that is the most stupid thing for the mind to do: to discipline itself to be quiet. Now seeing all that—actually seeing it, not as something theoretical—then there is an action from that perception; that very perception is the action of liberation from fear. So, on the occasion of any fear arising, there is immediate perception and the ending of it.

What is love? For most of us it is pleasure and hence fear; that is what we call love. When there is the understanding of fear and pleasure, then what is love? And "who" is going to answer this question?—the speaker, the priest, the book? Is some outside agency going to tell us we are doing marvelously well, carry on? Or, is it that having examined, observed, seen nonanalytically, the whole structure and nature of pleasure, fear, pain, we find that the "observer," the "thinker" is part of thought. *If there is no thinking there is no "thinker," the two are inseparable; the thinker is the thought.* There is a beauty and subtlety in seeing that. And where then is the mind that started to inquire into this question of fear?—you understand? What is the state of the mind now that it has gone through all this? Is it the same as it was before it came to this state? It has seen this thing very intimately, it has seen the nature of this thing called thought, fear and pleasure, it has seen all that; what is its actual state now? Obviously nobody can answer that except yourself; if you have actually gone into it, you will see that it has become completely transformed.

Questioner: (Inaudible)

Krishnamurti: It is one of the easiest things to ask a question. Probably some of us have been thinking what our question will be while the speaker was going on. We are more concerned with our question than with listening. One has to ask questions of oneself, not only here but everywhere. To ask the "right" question is far more important than to receive the answer. The solution of a problem lies in the understanding of the problem; the answer is not outside the problem, it is in the problem. One cannot look at the problem very clearly if one is concerned with the answer, with the solution. Most of us are so eager to resolve the problem without looking into it—and to look into it one has to have energy, intensity, a passion; not indolence and laziness as most of us have—we would rather somebody else solved it. There is nobody who is going to solve any of our problems, either political, religious or psychological. One has to have a great deal of vitality and passion, intensity, to look at and to observe the problem and then, as you observe, the answer is there very clearly.

This does not mean that you must not ask questions; on the contrary you must ask questions; you must doubt everything everybody has said, including the speaker.

Questioner: Is there a danger of introspection in looking into personal problems?

Krishnamurti: Why shouldn't there be danger? To cross the street there is a danger. Do you mean to say, we must not look because it is dangerous to look? I remember once —if I may repeat an incident—a very rich man came to see us and he said, "I am very, very serious and concerned with what you are talking about and I want to resolve all my 'so and so' "—you know, the nonsense that people talk about. I said, "All right, Sir, let us go into it," and we talked. He came several times, and after the second week he came to me and he said, "I am having dreadful dreams, frightening dreams, I seem to see everything around me disappearing, all kinds of things go"; and then he said, "Probably this is the result of my inquiry into myself and I see the danger of it"; after that he did not come any more.

We all want to be safe; we all want to be secure in our petty little world, the world of "well-established order" which is disorder, the world of our particular relationships, which we do not want to be disturbed—the relationship between wife and husband in which they hold together tight, in which there is misery, distrust, fear, in which there is danger, jealousy, anger, domination.

There is a way of looking into ourselves without fear, without danger; it is to look without any condemnation, without any justification, just to look, not to interpret, not to judge, not to evaluate. To do that the mind must be eager to learn in its observation of what actually is. What is the danger in "what is"? Human beings are violent; that is actually "what is"; and the danger they have brought about in this world is the result of this violence, it is the outcome of fear. What is there dangerous about observing it and trying to completely eradicate that fear? —that we may bring about a different society, different values? There is a great beauty in observation, in seeing things as they are, psychologically, inwardly; which does not mean that one accepts things as they are; which does not mean that one rejects or wants to do something about "what is"; the very perception of "what is" brings about its own mutation. But one must know the art of "looking" and the art of "looking" is never the introspective art, or the analytical art, but just observing without any choice.

11

Questioner: Is there not spontaneous fear?

Krishnamurti: Would you call that fear? When you know fire burns, when you see a precipice, is it fear to jump away from it? When you see a wild animal, a snake—to withdraw, is that fear?—or is it intelligence? That intelligence may be the result of conditioning, because you have been conditioned to the dangers of a precipice, for if you were not you could fall and that would be the end. Your intelligence tells you to be careful; is that intelligence fear? But is it intelligence that operates when we divide ourselves into nationalities, into religious groups?—when we make this division between you and me, we and they, is that intelligence? That which is in operation in such division, which brings about danger, which divides people, which brings war, is that intelligence operating or is it fear? There it is fear, not intelligence. In other words we have fragmented ourselves; part of us acts, where necessary, intelligently, as in avoiding a precipice, or a bus going by; but we are not intelligent enough to see the dangers of nationalism, the dangers of division between people. So one part of us—a very small part of us—is intelligent, the rest of us is not. Where there is fragmentation there must be conflict, there must be misery; the very essence of conflict is the division, the contradiction in us. That contradiction is not to be integrated. It is one of our peculiar idiosyncrasies that we must integrate ourselves. I do not know what it really means. Who is it that is going to integrate the two divided, opposed, natures? For is not the integrator himself part of that division? But when one sees the totality of it, when one has the perception of it, without any choice—there is no division.

Questioner: Is there any difference between correct thought and correct action?

Krishnamurti: When you use that word "correct," between thought and action, then that "correct" action is "incorrect" action—isn't it? When you use that word "correct" you have already an *idea* of what is correct. When you have an idea of what is "correct" it is "incorrect," because that "correct" is based on your prejudice, on your conditioning, on your fear, on your culture, on your society, on your own particular idiosyncrasies, fears, religious sanctions and so on. You have the norm, the pattern: that very pattern is in itself incorrect, is immoral. The social morality is immoral. Do you agree to that? If you do, then you have rejected social morality, which means greed, envy, ambition, nationality, the worship of class, all the rest of it. But have you, when you say "yes"? Social morality is immoral—do you really mean it?—or is it just a lot of words? Sir, to be really moral, virtuous, is one of the most extraordinary things in life; and that morality has nothing whatsoever to do with social, environmental behavior. One must be free to be really virtuous, and you are not free if you follow the social morality of greed, envy, competition, worship of success—you know all those things that are put forward by the church and by society as being moral.

Questioner: Do we have to wait for this to happen or is there some discipline we can use?

Krishnamurti: Must we have a discipline to realize that the very seeing is action? Must we?

Questioner: Would you talk about the quiet mind—is it the result of discipline? Or is it not?

Krishnamurti: Sir, look: a soldier on the parade ground, he is very quiet, with a straight back, holding the rifle very exactly; he is drilled, drilled day after day, day after day; any freedom is destroyed for him. He is very quiet; but is that quietness? Or when a child is absorbed in a toy, is that quietness?—remove the toy and the boy becomes what he is. So, will discipline (do understand this, Sir,

13

once and for all, it is so simple) will discipline bring about quietness? It may bring about dullness, a state of stagnancy, but does it bring about quietness in the sense, intensely active, yet quiet?

Questioner: Sir, what do you want us people here in this world to do?

Krishnamurti: Very simple, Sir: I don't want anything. That's first. Second: live, live in this world. This world is so marvelously beautiful. It is our world, our earth to live upon, but we do not live, we are narrow, we are separate, we are anxious, we are frightened human beings, and therefore we do not live, we have no relationship, we are isolated, despairing human beings. We do not know what it means to live in that ecstatic, blissful sense. I say one can live that way only when one knows how to be free from all the stupidities of one's life. To be free from them is only possible in becoming aware of one's relationship, not only with human beings, but with ideas, with nature, with everything. In that relationship one discovers what one is, one's fear, anxiety, despair, loneliness, one's utter lack of love. One is full of theories, words, knowledge of what other people have said; one knows nothing about oneself, and therefore one does not know how to live.

Questioner: How do you explain different levels of consciousness in terms of the human brain? The brain seems to be a physical affair, the mind does not seem to be a physical affair. In addition, the mind seems to have a conscious part and an unconscious part. How can we see with any clarity in all these different ideas?

Krishnamurti: What is the difference between the mind and the brain; is that it, Sir? The actual physical brain, which is the result of the past, which is the outcome of evolution, of many thousand yesterdays, with all its memories and knowledge and experience, is not that brain part

14

of the total mind?—the mind in which there is a conscious level and the unconscious level? The physical as well as the nonphysical, the psychological, isn't all that one whole? —is it not we who have divided it as the conscious and unconscious, the brain and the not brain? Can we not look at the whole thing as a totality, nonfragmented?

Is the unconscious so very different from the conscious? Or is it not part of the totality, but we have divided it? From that arises the question: how is the conscious mind to be aware of the unconscious? Can the positive which is the operative—the thing that is working all day—can that observe the unconscious?

I do not know if we have time to go into this. Are you not tired? Please, sirs, do not reduce this to an entertainment, as one can, sitting in a nice warm room, listening to some voice. We are dealing with very serious things, and if you have worked, as one should have, then you must be tired. The brain cannot take more than a certain amount, and to go into this question of the unconscious and the conscious requires a very sharp, clear mind to observe. I doubt very much if at the end of an hour and a half you are capable of it. So may we, if you agree, take up this question later?

London, March 16, 1969

15

2. Fragmentation

**Division. The conscious
and the unconscious.
Dying to the "known."**

We were going to talk over this evening the question of
the conscious and unconscious, the superficial mind and
the deeper layers of consciousness. I wonder why we divide life into fragments, the business life, social life, family
life, religious life, the life of sport and so on? Why is
there this division, not only in ourselves but also socially
—we and they, you and me, love and hate, dying and
living? I think we ought to go into this question rather
deeply to find out if there is a way of life in which there
is no division at all between living and dying, between
the conscious and the unconscious, the business and social
life, the family life and the individual life.

These divisions between nationalities, religions, classes,
all this separation in oneself in which there is so much
contradiction—why do we live that way? It breeds such
turmoil, conflict, war; it brings about real insecurity, outwardly as well as inwardly. There is so much division, as
God and the devil, the good and the bad, "what should
be" and "what is."

I think it would be worthwhile to spend this evening in
trying to find out if there is a way of living—not theoretically or intellectually but actually—a way of life, in which
there is no division whatsoever; a way of life in which action is not fragmented, so that it is one constant flow,
where every action is related to all other actions.

16

To find a way of living in which there is no fragmentation one has to go very deeply into the question of love and death; in understanding that we may be able to come upon a way of life that is a continuous movement, not broken up, a way of life that is highly intelligent. A fragmented mind lacks intelligence; the man who leads half a dozen lives—which is accepted as being highly moral— obviously shows lack of intelligence.

It seems to me that the idea of integration—of putting together the various fragments to make a whole—is obviously not intelligent, for it implies that there is an integrator, one who is integrating, putting together, all the fragments; but the very entity that tries to do this is also part of that fragment.

What is needed is such intelligence and passion as to bring about a radical revolution in one's life, so that there is no contradictory action but whole, continuous movement. To bring about this change in one's life there must be passion. If one is to do anything worthwhile, one must have this intense passion—which is not pleasure. To understand that action in which there is no fragmentation or contradiction, there must be this passion. Intellectual concepts and formulas will not change one's way of life, but only the very understanding of "what is"; and for that there must be an intensity, a passion.

To find out if there is a way of living—daily living, not a monastic living—which has this quality of passion and intelligence one has to understand the nature of pleasure. We went into the question of pleasure the other day, of how thought sustains an experience, which has given for the moment a delight, and how by thinking about it pleasure is sustained; where there is pleasure there is bound to be pain and fear. Is love pleasure? For most of us moral values are based on pleasure; the very sacrificing of oneself, controlling oneself in order to conform, is the urge of pleasure—greater, nobler, or whatever it is. Is love a thing of pleasure? Again that word "love" is so loaded, everyone uses it, from the politician to the husband and wife. And it seems to me that it is only love, in the deepest sense of the word, that can bring about a way of life in which there is no fragmentation at all. Fear is always part of pleasure; obviously where there is any kind of fear in relationship there must be fragmentation, there must be division.

It is really quite a deep issue, this inquiry as to why the human mind has always divided itself in opposition to others, resulting in violence and what it is hoped to achieve through violence. We human beings are committed to a way of life that leads to war and yet at the same time we want peace, we want freedom; but it is peace only as an idea, as an ideology; and at the same time everything that we do conditions us.

There is the division, psychologically, of time; time as the past (the yesterday), today and tomorrow; we must inquire into this if we are to find a way of life in which division does not exist at all. We have to consider if it is time, as the past, the present and the future—psychological time—that is the cause of this division. Is division brought about by the known, as memory, which is the past, which is the content of the brain itself? Or does division arise because the "observer," the "experiencer," the "thinker" is always separate from the thing which he observes, experiences? Or is it the egotistic self-centered activity, which is the "me" and the "you," creating its own resistances, its own isolated activities, which causes this division? In going into this, one must be aware of all these issues: time; the "observer" separating himself from the thing observed; the experiencer different from the experience; pleasure; and whether all this has anything whatsoever to do with love.

Is there tomorrow psychologically?—actually, not invented by thought. There is a tomorrow in chronological time; but is there actually tomorrow, psychologically, inwardly? If there is tomorrow as idea, then action is not complete, and that action brings about division, contradiction. The idea of tomorrow, the future is—is it not?—the cause of not seeing things very clearly as they are now

—"I hope to see them more clearly tomorrow." One is lazy; one does not have this passion, this vital interest, to find out. Thought invents the idea of eventually arriving, eventually understanding; so for that, time is necessary, many days are necessary. Does time bring understanding, does it enable one to see something very clearly?

Is it possible for the mind to be free of the past so that it is not bound by time? Tomorrow, psychologically, is in terms of the known; is there then the possibility of being free from the known? Is there the possibility of an action not in terms of the known?

One of the most difficult things is to communicate. There must be verbal communication, obviously, but I think there is a much deeper level of communication, which is not only a verbal communication but communion, where both of us meet at the same level, with the same intensity, with the same passion; then only does communion take place, something far more important than mere verbal communication. And as we are talking about something rather complex, which touches very deeply our daily life, there must not only be verbal communication but also communion. What we are concerned about is a radical revolution, psychologically; not in some distant future, but actually today, now. We are concerned to find out whether the human mind, which has been so conditioned, can change immediately, so that its actions are a continuous whole, not broken up, and therefore pitted with its regrets, despairs, pains, fears, anxieties, its guilt and so on. How can the mind throw it all off and be completely fresh, young and innocent? That is really the issue. I do not think this is possible—such a radical revolution—so long as there is a division between the "observer" and the observed, between the "experiencer" and the experienced. It is this division that brings about conflict. All division must bring about conflict, and through conflict, through struggle, through battle, obviously there can be no change, in the deep psychological sense—though there may be superficial changes. So how is the mind, the heart and the brain, the total state, to cope with this problem of division?

We said we would go into this question of the conscious and the deeper levels, the unconscious: and we are asking why is there this division, this division between the conscious mind, occupied with its own daily activities, worries, problems, superficial pleasures, earning a livelihood and so on and the deeper levels of that mind, with all its hidden motives, its drives, compulsive demands, its fears? Why is there this division? Does it exist because we are so occupied, superficially, with endless chatter, with the constant demand, superficially, for amusement, entertainment, religious as well as otherwise? Because the superficial mind cannot possibly delve, go deeply, into itself while this division arises.

What is the content of the deeper layers of the mind? —not according to the psychologists, Freud and so on— and how do you find out, if you do not read what others have said? How will you find out what your unconscious is? You will watch it, will you not? Or, will you expect your dreams to interpret the contents of the unconscious? And who is to translate those dreams? The experts?—they are also conditioned by their specialization. And one asks: is it possible not to dream at all?—excepting of course for nightmares when one has eaten the wrong food, or has had too heavy a meal in the evening.

There is—we will use the word for the time being—the unconscious. What is it made of?—obviously the past; all the racial consciousness, the racial residue, the family tradition, the various religious and social conditioning— hidden, dark, undiscovered; can all that be discovered and exposed without dreams?—or without going to an analyst?—so that the mind, when it does sleep, is quiet, not incessantly active. And, because it is quiet, may there not come into it quite a different quality, a different activity altogether, dissociated from the daily anxieties, fears, worries, problems, demands? To find that out—if that is possible—that is, not to dream at all, so that the mind is really fresh when it wakes up in the morning, one has to be aware during the day, aware of the hints and intimations. Those one can discover only in relationship; when you are watching your relationship with others, without condemning, judging, evaluating; just watching how you behave, your reactions; seeing without any choice; just observing, so that during the day the hidden, the unconscious, is exposed.

Why do we give such deep significance and meaning to the unconscious?—for after all, it is as trivial as the conscious. If the conscious mind is extraordinarily active, watching, listening, seeing, then the conscious mind becomes far more important than the unconscious; in that state all the contents of the unconscious are exposed; the division between the various layers comes to an end. Watching your reactions when you sit in a bus, when you are talking to your wife, your husband, when in your office, writing, being alone—if you are ever alone—then this whole process of observation, this act of seeing (in which there is no division as the "observer" and the "observed") ends the contradiction.

When this is somewhat clear, then we can ask: What is love? Is love pleasure? Is love jealousy? Is love possessive? Does love dominate?—the husband over the wife and the wife over the husband. Surely, not one of these things is love; yet we are burdened with all these things, and yet we say to our husband or our wife, or whoever it is, "I love you." Now, most of us are, in some form or other, envious. Envy arises through comparison, through measurement, through wanting to be something different from what one is. Can we see envy as it actually is, and be entirely free of it, for it never to happen again?—otherwise love cannot exist. Love is not of time; love cannot be cultivated; it is not a thing of pleasure.

What is death?—What is the relationship between love and death? I think we will find the relationship between the two when we understand the meaning of "death"; to understand that we must obviously understand what living is. What actually is our living?—the daily living, not the ideological, the intellectual something, which we consider should be, but which is really false. What actually is our living?—the daily living of conflict, despair, loneliness, isolation. Our life is a battlefield, sleeping and waking; we try to escape from this in various ways through music, art, museums, religious or philosophical entertainment, spinning a lot of theories, caught up in knowledge, anything but putting an end to this conflict, to this battle which we call living, with its constant sorrow.

Can the sorrow in daily life end? Unless the mind changes radically our living has very little meaning—going to the office every day, earning a livelihood, reading a few books, being able to quote cleverly, being very well informed—a life which is empty, a real bourgeois life. And then as one becomes aware of this state of affairs, one begins to invent a meaning to life; find some significance to give to it; one searches out the clever people who will give one the significance, the purpose, of life—which is another escape from living. This kind of living must undergo a radical transformation.

Why is it we are frightened of death?—as most people are. Frightened of what? Do please observe your own fears of what we call death—being frightened of coming to the end of this battle which we call living. We are frightened of the unknown, what might happen; we are frightened of leaving the known things, the family, the books, the attachment to your house and furniture, to the people near us. We are frightened to let go of the things known; and the known is this living in sorrow, pain and despair, with occasional flashes of joy; there is no end to this constant struggle; that is what we call living—of that we are frightened to let go. Is it the "me"—who is the result of all this accumulation—that is frightened that it will come to an end?—therefore it demands a future hope, therefore there must be reincarnation. The idea of reincarnation, in which the whole of the East believes, is that you will be born next life a little higher up on the rungs of the ladder. You have been a dishwasher this life, next life you will be a prince, or whatever it is—somebody else will go and wash the dishes for you. For those who believe in reincarnation, what you are in this life matters very much, because what you do, how you behave, what your thoughts are, what your activities are, so in the next life depending on this, you either get a reward or you are punished. But they do not care a pin about how they behave; for them it is just another form of belief, just as the belief that there is heaven, God, what you will. Actually all that matters is what you are now, today, how you actually behave, not only outwardly but inwardly. The West has its own form of consolation about death, it rationalizes it, it has its own religious conditioning.

So, what is death, actually—the ending? The organism is going to end, because it grows old, or from disease and accident. Very few of us grow old beautifully because we are tortured entities, our faces show it as we grow older —and there is the sadness of old age, remembering the things of the past.

Can one die to everything that is "known," psychologically, from day to day? Unless there is freedom from that "known" what is "possible" can never be captured. As it is, our "possibility" is always within the field of the "known"; but when there is freedom, then that "possibility" is immense. Can one die, psychologically, to all one's past, to all the attachments, fears, to the anxiety, vanity, and pride, so completely that tomorrow you wake up a fresh human being? You will say, "How is this to be done, what is the method?" There is no method, because "a method" implies tomorrow; it implies that you will practice and achieve something eventually, tomorrow, after many tomorrows. But can you see immediately the truth of it—see it actually, not theoretically—that the mind cannot be fresh, innocent, young, vital, passionate, unless there is an ending, psychologically, to everything of the past? But we do not want to let the past go because we

23

are the past; all our thoughts are based on the past; all knowledge is the past; so the mind cannot let go; any effort it makes to let go is still part of the past, the past hoping to achieve a different state.

The mind must become extraordinarily quiet, silent; and it does become extraordinarily quiet without any resistance, without any system, when it sees this whole issue. Man has always sought immortality; he paints a picture, puts his name on it, that is a form of immortality; leaving a name behind, man always wants to leave something of himself behind. What has he got to give—apart from technological knowledge—what has he of himself to give? What is he? You and I, what are we, psychologically? You may have a bigger bank account, be cleverer than I am, or this and that; but psychologically, what are we?—a lot of words, memories, experiences, and these we want to hand over to a son, put in a book, or paint in a picture, "me." The "me" becomes extremely important, the "me" opposed to the community, the "me" wanting to identify itself, wanting to fulfill itself, wanting to become something great—you know, all the rest of it. When you observe that "me," you see that it is a bundle of memories, empty words: that is what we cling to; that is the very essence of the separation between you and me, they and we.

When you understand all this—observe it, not through another but through yourself, watch it very closely, without any judgment, evaluation, suppression, just to observe—then you will see that love is only possible when there is death. Love is not memory, love is not pleasure. It is said that love is related to sex—back again to the division between profane love and sacred love, with approval of one and condemnation of the other. Surely, love is none of these things. One cannot come upon it, totally, completely, unless there is a dying to the past, a dying to all the travail, conflict and sorrow; then there is love; then one can do what one will.

As we said the other day, it is fairly easy to ask a question; but ask it purposefully and keep with it until you have resolved it totally for yourself; such asking has an importance; but to ask casually has very little meaning.

Questioner: If you do not have the division between the "what is" and the "what should be" you might become complacent, you would not worry about the terrible things that are going on.

Krishnamurti: What is the reality of "what should be"? Has it any reality at all? Man is violent but the "should be" peaceful. What is the reality of the "should be," and why do we have the "should be"? If this division were to cease, would man become complacent, accept everything? Would I accept violence if I had no ideal of nonviolence? Nonviolence has been preached from the most ancient days: don't kill, be compassionate, and so on; and the fact is, man is violent, that is "what is." If man accepts it as inevitable, then he becomes complacent—as he is now. He has accepted war as a way of life and he goes on, though a thousand sanctions, religious, social, and otherwise, say, "Do not kill"—not only man, but animals; but he does kill animals for food, and he does go to war. So if there was no ideal at all you would be left with "what is." Would that make one complacent? Or would you then have the energy, the interest, the vitality, to solve "what is"? Is not the ideal of nonviolence an escape from the fact of violence? When the mind is not escaping, but is confronted with the fact of violence—that it is violent, not condemning it, not judging it—then surely, such a mind has an entirely different quality and there is no longer violence. Such a mind does not accept violence; violence is not merely hurting or killing somebody; violence is equally this distortion, in conforming, imitating, following the social morality, or following one's own peculiar morality. Every form of control and suppression is a form of distortion and therefore violence. Surely, to understand "what is," there must be a tension, a watchfulness to find

25

out what actually is. What actually is, is the division man has created by nationalism, which is one of the major causes of war; we accept it, we worship the flag; and there are the divisions created by religion, we are Christians, Buddhists, this or that. Can we not be free of the "what is" by observing the actual fact? You can only be free of it when the mind does not distort what is observed.

Questioner: What is the difference between conceptual seeing and actual seeing?

Krishnamurti: Do you see a tree conceptually or actually? When you see a flower, do you see it directly, or do you see it through the screen of your particular knowledge, botanical or nonbotanical, or through the pleasure it gives? How do you see it? If it is conceptual seeing, that is to say, it is seen through thought, is it seen? Do you see your wife or your husband?—or do you see the image you have about him or her? That image is the concept through which you see conceptually; but when there is no image at all then you actually see, then you are actually related.

So, what is the mechanism that builds the image, that prevents us from actually seeing the tree, the wife, or the husband, or the friend, or whatever it is? Obviously—although I hope I am wrong—you have an image about me, about the speaker—no? If you have an image about the speaker, you are really not listening to the speaker at all. And when you look at your wife, or your husband, and so on, and you look through an image, you are not actually seeing the person, you are seeing the person through the image, and therefore there is no relationship at all; you may say "I love you," but it has no meaning at all.

Can the mind stop forming images?—in the sense of which we are speaking. It is only possible when the mind is completely attentive at the moment, at the instant of the challenge or the impression. To take a very simple example: you are flattered, you like that, and the very "like" builds the image. But if you listen to that flattery with complete attention, neither liking nor disliking, listen to it completely, wholly, then an image is not formed; you do not call him your friend, and alternatively, the person who insults you, you do not call him your enemy. "Image forming" arises from inattention; when there is attention there is no building up of any concept. Do it; one finds out, very simply. When you give complete attention to looking at a tree, or a flower or a cloud, then there is no projection of your botanical knowledge, or your like or dislike, you just look—which does not mean that you identify yourself with the tree, you cannot become the tree anyhow. If you look at your wife, husband or friend without any image, then relationship is something entirely different; then thought does not come into it at all and there is a possibility of love.

Questioner: Are love and freedom concomitant?

Krishnamurti: Can we love without freedom? If we are not free, can we love? If we are jealous, can we love? Frightened, can we love? Or, if we are pursuing our own particular ambition in the office and we come home and say "I love you, darling"—is that love? In the office we are brutal, cunning, and at home we try to be docile, loving—is that possible? With one hand kill, with the other hand love? Can the ambitious man ever love, or the competitive man ever know what love means? We accept all these things and social morality; but when we deny that social morality, completely, with all our being, then we are really moral—but we do not do that. We are socially, morally, respectable, therefore we do not know what love is. Without love we can never find out what truth is, nor find out if there is such a thing—or not such a thing—as God. We can only know what love is when we know how to die to everything of yesterday, to all the images of pleasure, sexual or otherwise; then, when there is love, which in itself is virtue, which in itself is morality—all ethics are in it—then only does that reality, that something which is not measurable, come into being.

Questioner: The individual, being in turmoil, creates society; to change society are you advocating that the individual detach himself, so as not to depend on society?

Krishnamurti: Is not the individual the society? You and I have created this society, with our greed, with our ambition, with our nationalism, with our competitiveness, brutality, violence; that is what we have done outwardly, because that is what we are inwardly. The war that is going on in Vietnam, for that we are responsible, you and I, actually, because we have accepted war as the way of life. Are you suggesting that we detach ourselves? On the contrary, how can you detach yourself from yourself? You are part of this whole mess and can only be free of this ugliness, this violence, everything that is actually there, not by detachment, but by learning, by watching, by understanding the whole thing in yourself and thereby being free of all the violence. You cannot detach yourself from yourself; and this gives rise to the problem of "who" is to do it. "Who" is to detach "me" from society, or "me" from myself? The entity who wants to detach himself, is he not part of the whole circus? To understand all this— that the "observer" is not different from the thing observed—is meditation; it requires a great deal of penetration into oneself, nonanalytically; by observing in relationship with things, with property, with people, with ideas, with nature, one comes upon this sense of complete freedom inwardly.

London, March 20, 1969

3. Meditation

The meaning of "search."
Problems involved in practice and control.
The quality of silence.

I should like to talk about something which I think is very important; in the understanding of it we shall, perhaps, be able to have for ourselves a total perception of life without any fragmentation, so that we may act totally, freely, happily.

We are always seeking some form of mystery because we are so dissatisfied with the life we lead, with the shallowness of our activities, which have very little meaning and to which we try to give significance, a meaning; but this is an intellectual act which therefore remains superficial, tricky and in the end meaningless. And yet knowing all this—knowing our pleasures are very soon over, our everyday activities are routine; knowing also that our problems, so many of them, can perhaps never be solved; not believing in anything, nor having faith in traditional values, in the teachers, in the gurus, in the sanctions of the Church or society—knowing all this, most of us are always probing or seeking, trying to find out something really worthwhile, something that is not touched by thought, something that really has an extraordinary sense of beauty and ecstasy. Most of us, I think, are trying to seek out something that is enduring, that is not easily made corrupt. We put aside the obvious and there is a deep longing—not emotional or sentimental—a deep inquiry which might open the door to something that is not measured by thought, something that cannot be put into any category of faith or belief. But is there any meaning to searching, to seeking?

We are going to discuss the question of meditation; it is a rather complex question and before we go into it, we have to be very clear about this searching, this seeking for experience, trying to find out a reality. We have to understand the meaning of seeking and the searching out of truth, the intellectual groping after something new, which is not of time, which is not brought about by one's demands, compulsions and despair. Is truth ever to be found by seeking? Is it recognizable when one has found it? If one has, can one say, "This is the truth"—"This is the real"? Has search any meaning at all? Most religious people are always talking about seeking truth; and we are asking if truth can ever be sought after. In the idea of seeking, of finding, is there not also the idea of recognition—the idea that if I find something I must be able to recognize it? Does not recognition imply that I have already known it? Is truth "recognizable"—in the sense of its having already been experienced, so that one is able to say, "This is it"? So what is the value of seeking at all? Or, if there is no value in it, then is there value only in constant observation, constant listening?—which is not the same as seeking. When there is constant observation there is no movement of the past. "To observe" implies seeing very clearly; to see very clearly there must be freedom, freedom from resentment, freedom from enmity, from any prejudice or grudge, freedom from all those memories that one has stored up as knowledge, which interfere with seeing. When there is that quality, that kind of freedom with constant observation—not only of the things outside but also inwardly—of what is actually going on, what then is the need of seeking at all?—for it is all there, the fact, the "what is," it is observed. But the moment we want to change "what is" into something else, the process of distortion takes place. Observing freely, without any distortion, without any evaluation, without any desire for pleasure, in just observing, we see that "what is" undergoes an extraordinary change.

Most of us try to fill our life with knowledge, with entertainment, with spiritual aspirations and beliefs, which, as we observe, have very little value; we want to experience something transcendental, something beyond all worldly things, we want to experience something immense, that has no borders, that has no time. To "experience" something immeasurable one must understand the implications of "experience." Why do we want "experience" at all?

Please do not accept or deny what the speaker is saying, just examine it. The speaker—let us again be definite about that matter—has no value whatsoever. (It's like the telephone, you do not obey what the telephone says. The telephone has no authority, but you listen to it.) If you listen with care, there is in that, affection, not agreement or disagreement, but a quality of mind that says, "Let's see what you're talking about, let us see if it has any value at all, let us see what is true and what is false." Do not accept or deny, but observe and listen, not only to what is being said, but also to your reactions, to your distortions, as you are listening; see your prejudices, your opinions, your images, your experiences, see how they are going to prevent you from listening.

We are asking: what is the significance of experience? Has it any significance? Can experience wake up a mind that is asleep, that has come to certain conclusions and is held and conditioned by beliefs? Can experience wake it up, shatter all that structure? Can such a mind—so conditioned, so burdened by its own innumerable problems and despairs and sorrows—respond to any challenge?—can it? And if it does respond, must not the response be inadequate and therefore lead to more conflict? Always to seek for wider, deeper, transcendental experience, is a form of escape from the actual reality of "what is," which is ourselves, our own conditioned mind. A mind that is extraordinarily awake, intelligent, free, why should it need, why should it have, any "experience" at all? Light is light, it does not ask for more light. The desire for more "experience" is escape from the actual, the "what is."

If one is free from this everlasting search, free from the demand and the desire to experience something extraordinary, then we can proceed to find out what meditation is. That word—like the words "love," "death," "beauty," "happiness"—is so loaded. There are so many schools which teach you how to meditate. But to understand what meditation is, one must lay the foundation of righteous behavior. Without that foundation, meditation is really a form of self-hypnosis; without being free from anger, jealousy, envy, greed, acquisitiveness, hate, competition, the desire for success—all the moral, respectable forms of what is considered righteous—without laying the right foundation, without actually living a daily life free of the distortion of personal fear, anxiety, greed and so on, meditation has very little meaning. The laying of that foundation is all-important. So one asks: what is virtue? What is morality? Please do not say that this question is bourgeois, that is has no meaning in a society which is permissive, which allows anything. We are not concerned with that kind of society; we are concerned with a life completely free from fear, a life which is capable of deep, abiding love. Without that, meditation becomes a deviation; it is like taking a drug—as so many have done—to have an extraordinary experience and yet leading a shoddy little life. Those who take drugs do have some strange experiences, they see perhaps a little more color, they become perhaps a little more sensitive, and being sensitive, in that chemical state, they do perhaps see things without space between the "observer" and the thing observed; but when the chemical effect is over, they are back to where they were with fear, with boredom, back again in the old routine—so they have to take the drug again.

Unless one lays the foundation of virtue, meditation becomes a trick to control the mind, to make the mind quiet, to force the mind to conform to the pattern of a system that says, "Do these things and you will have great reward." But such a mind—do what you will with all the methods and the systems that are offered—will remain small, petty, conditioned, and therefore worthless. One has to inquire into what virtue is, what behavior is. Is behavior the result of environmental conditioning, of a society, of a culture, in which one has been brought up?—you behave according to that. Is that virtue? Or does virtue lie in freedom from the social morality of greed, envy and all the rest of it?—which is considered highly respectable. Can virtue be cultivated?—and if it can be cultivated then does it not become a mechanical thing and therefore have no virtue at all? Virtue is something that is living, flowing, that is constantly renewing itself, it cannot possibly be put together in time; it is like suggesting that you can cultivate humility. Can you cultivate humility? It is only the vain man that "cultivates" humility; whatever he may cultivate he will still remain vain. But in seeing very clearly the nature of vanity and pride, in that very seeing there is freedom from that vanity and pride—and in that there is humility. When this is very clear then we can proceed to find out what meditation is. If one cannot do this very deeply, in a most real and serious way—not just for one or two days then drop it—please do not talk about meditation. Meditation, if you understand what it is, is one of the most extraordinary things; but you cannot possibly understand it unless you have come to the end of seeking, groping, wanting, greedily clutching at something which you consider truth—which is your own projection. You cannot come to it unless you are no longer demanding "experience" at all, but are understanding the confusion in which one lives, the disorder of one's own life. In the observation of that disorder, order comes—which is not a blueprint. When you have done this—which in itself is meditation—then we can ask, not only what meditation is, but also what meditation is not, because in the denial of that which is false, the truth is.

Any system, any method, that teaches you how to meditate is obviously false. One can see why, intellectually, logically, for if you practice something according to a method—however noble, however ancient, however modern, however popular—you are making yourself mechanical, you are doing something over and over again in order to achieve something. In meditation the end is not different from the means. But the method promises you something; it is a means to an end. If the means is mechanical, then the end is also something brought about by the machine; the mechanical mind says, "I'll get something." One has to be completely free from all methods, all systems; that is already the beginning of meditation; you are already denying something which is utterly false and meaningless. And again, there are those who practice "awareness." Can you practice awareness?—if you are "practicing" awareness, then you are all the time being inattentive. So, be aware of inattention, not practice how to be attentive; if you are aware of your inattention, out of that awareness there is attention, you do not have to practice it. Do please understand this, it is so clear and so simple. You do not have to go to Burma, China, India, places which are romantic but not factual. I remember once traveling in a car, in India, with a group of people. I was sitting in front with the driver, there were three behind who were talking about awareness, wanting to discuss with me what awareness is. The car was going very fast. A goat was in the road and the driver did not pay much attention and ran over the poor animal. The gentlemen behind were discussing what is awareness; they never knew what had happened! You laugh; but that is what we are all doing, we are intellectually concerned with the idea of awareness, the verbal, dialectical investigation of opinion, yet not actually aware of what is taking place.

There is no practice, only the living thing. And there comes the question: how is thought to be controlled? Thought wanders all over the place; you want to think about something, it is off on something else. They say practice, control; think about a picture, a sentence, or whatever it is, concentrate; thought buzzes off in another direction, so you pull it back and this battle goes on, backward and forward. So one asks: what is the need for control of thought at all and who is the entity that is going to control thought? Please follow this closely. Unless one understands this real question, one will not be able to see what meditation means. When one says, "I must control thought," who is the controller, the censor? Is the censor different from the thing he wants to control, shape or change into a different quality?—are they not both the same? What happens when the "thinker" sees that he is the thought—which he is—that the "experiencer" is the experience? Then what is one to do? Are you following the question? The thinker is the thought and thought wanders off; then the thinker, thinking he is separate, says, "I must control it." Is the thinker different from the thing called thought? If there is no thought, is there a thinker?

What takes place when the thinker sees he is the thought? What actually takes place when the "thinker" is the thought, as the "observer" is the observed? What takes place? In that there is no separation, no division and therefore no conflict; therefore thought is no longer to be controlled, shaped; then, what takes place? Is there then any wandering of thought at all? Before, there was control of thought, there was concentration of thought, there was the conflict between the "thinker," who wanted to control thought, and thought wandering off. That goes on all the time with all of us. Then there is the sudden realization that the "thinker" is the thought—a realization, not a verbal statement, but an actuality. Then what takes place? Is there such a thing as thought wandering? It is only when the "observer" is different from thought that he censors it; then he can say, "This is right or this is wrong thought," or "Thought is wandering away. I must control it." But when the thinker realizes that he is the thought, is there a wandering at all? Go into it, sirs, don't accept it, you will see it for yourself. It is only when there is a resistance that there is conflict; the resistance is created by the thinker who thinks he is separate from the thought; but when the thinker realizes that he is the thought, there is no resistance—which does not mean that thought goes all over the place and does what it likes, on the contrary.

The whole concept of control and concentration undergoes a tremendous change; it becomes attention, something entirely different. If one understands the nature of attention, that attention can be focused, one understands that it is quite different from concentration, which is exclusion. Then you will ask, "Can I do anything without concentration?" "Do I not need concentration in order to do anything?" But can you not do something with attention? —which is not concentration. "Attention" implies to attend, that is to listen, hear, see, with all the totality of your being, with your body, with your nerves, with your eyes, with your ears, with your mind, with your heart, completely. In that total attention—in which there is no division—you can do anything; and in such attention is no resistance. So then, the next thing is, can the mind in which is included the brain—the brain being conditioned, the brain being the result of thousands of thousands of years of evolution, the brain which is the storehouse of memory—can that become quiet? Because it is only when the total mind is silent, quiet, that there is perception, seeing clearly, with a mind that is not confused. How can the mind be quiet, be still? I do not know if you have seen for yourself that to look at a beautiful tree, or a cloud full of light and glory, you must look completely, silently, otherwise you are not looking directly at it, you are looking at it with some image of pleasure, or the memory of yesterday, you are not actually looking at it, you are looking at the image rather than at the fact.

So, one asks, can the totality of the mind, the brain included, be completely still? People have asked this question—really very serious people—they have not been able to solve it, they have tried tricks, they have said that the mind can be made still through the repetition of words. Have you ever tried it—repeating "Ave Maria," or those Sanskrit words that some people bring over from India, mantras—repeating certain words to make the mind still? It does not matter what word it is, make it rhythmic— Coca Cola, any word—repeat it often and you will see that your mind becomes quiet; but it is a dull mind, it is not a sensitive mind, alert, active, vital, passionate, intense. A dull mind though it may say, "I have had tremendous transcendental experience," is deceiving itself.

So it is not in the repetition of words, nor in trying to force it; too many tricks have been played upon the mind for it to be quiet; yet one knows deeply within oneself that when the mind is quiet then the whole thing is over, that then there is true perception.

How is the mind, the brain included, to be completely quiet? Some say breathe properly, take deep breaths, that is, get more oxygen into your blood; a shoddy little mind breathing very deeply, day after day, can be fairly quiet; but it is still what it is, a shoddy little mind. Or practice yoga?—again, so many things are involved in this. Yoga means skill in action, not merely the practice of certain exercises which are necessary to keep the body healthy, strong, sensitive—which includes eating the right food, not stuffing it with a lot of meat and so on (we won't go into all that, you are all probably meat eaters). Skill in action demands great sensitivity of the body, a lightness of the body, eating the right food, not what your tongue dictates, or what you are used to.

Then what is one to do? Who puts this question? One sees very clearly that our lives are in disorder, inwardly and outwardly; and yet order is necessary, as orderly as mathematical order and that can come about only by observing the disorder, not by trying to conform to the blueprint of what others may consider, or you yourself may consider, order. By seeing, by being aware of the disorder, out of that comes order. One also sees that the mind must be extraordinarily quiet, sensitive, alert, not caught in any habit, physical or psychological; how is that to come about? Who puts this question? Is the question put by the mind that chatters, the mind that has so much knowledge? Has it learned a new thing?—which is, "I can see very clearly only when I am quiet, therefore, I must be quiet." Then it says, "How am I to be quiet?" Surely such a question is wrong in itself; the moment it asks "how" it is looking for a system, therefore destroying the very thing that is being inquired into, which is: how can the mind be completely still?—not mechanically, not forced, not compelled to be still. A mind that is not compelled to be still is extraordinarily active, sensitive, alert. But when you ask "how" then there is the division between the observer and the thing observed.

When you realize that there is no method, no system, that no mantra, no teacher, nothing in the world that is going to help you to be quiet, when you realize the truth that it is only the quiet mind that sees, then the mind becomes extraordinarily quiet. It is like seeing danger and avoiding it; in the same way, seeing that the mind must be completely quiet, it is quiet.

Now the *quality* of silence matters. A very small mind can be very quiet, it has its little space in which to be quiet; that little space, with its little quietness, is the deadest thing—you know what it is. But a mind that has limitless space and that quietness, that stillness, has no center as the "me," the "observer," is quite different. In that silence there is no "observer" at all; that quality of silence has vast space, it is without border and intensely active; the activity of that silence is entirely different from the activity which is self-centered. If the mind has gone that far (and really it is not that far, it is always there if you know how to look), then perhaps that which man has sought throughout the centuries, God, truth, the immeasurable, the nameless, the timeless, is there—without your invitation, it is there. Such a man is blessed, there is truth for him and ecstasy.

Shall we talk this over, ask questions? You might say to me, "What value has all this in daily life? I've got to live, go to the office; there is the family, there is the boss, competition—what has all this got to do with it?" Do you not ask that question? If you ask it, then you have not followed all that has been said this morning. Meditation is not something different from daily life; do not go off into the corner of a room and meditate for ten minutes, then come out of it and be a butcher—both metaphorically and actually. Meditation is one of the most serious things; you do it all day, in the office, with the family, when you say to somebody, "I love you," when you are considering your children, when you educate them to become soldiers, to kill, to be nationalized, worshiping the flag, educating them to enter into this trap of the modern world; watching all that, realizing your part in it, all that is part of meditation. And when you so meditate you will find in it an extraordinary beauty; you will act rightly at every moment; and if you do not act rightly at a given moment it does not matter, you will pick it up again—you will not waste time in regret. Meditation is part of life, not something different from life.

Questioner: Can you say something about laziness?

Krishnamurti: Laziness—first of all, what is wrong with laziness? Do not let us confuse laziness with leisure. Most of us, unfortunately, are lazy and inclined to be indolent, so we whip ourselves to be active—therefore we become more lazy. The more I resist laziness the more I become lazy. But look at laziness, in the morning when I get up feeling terribly lazy, not wanting to do so many things. Why has the body become lazy?—probably one has overeaten, overindulged sexually, one has done everything the previous day and night to make the body heavy, dull; and the body says for God's sake leave me alone for a little while; and one wants to whip it, make it active; but one

39

does not correct the way of one's life, so one takes a pill to be active. But if one observes, one will see that the body has its own intelligence; it requires a great deal of intelligence to observe the intelligence of the body. One forces it, one drives it; one is used to meat, one drinks, smokes, you know all the rest of it and therefore the body itself loses its own intrinsic organic intelligence. To allow the body to act intelligently, the mind has to become intelligent and not allow itself to interfere with the body. You try it and you will see that laziness undergoes a tremendous change.

There is also the question of leisure. People are having more and more leisure, especially in the well-to-do societies. What does one do with the leisure?—that is becoming the problem: more amusement, more cinemas, more television, more books, more chatter, more boating, more cricket: you know, up and out, filling the leisure time with all kinds of activity. The Church says fill it with God, go to church, pray—all those tricks which they have done before, which is but another form of entertainment. Or one talks endlessly about this and that. You have leisure; will you use it to turn outwardly or inwardly? Life is not just the inward life; life is a movement, it is like the tide going out and coming in. What will you do with leisure? Become more learned, more able to quote books? Will you go out lecturing (which I do unfortunately), or go inwardly very deeply? To go inward very deeply, the outer must also be understood. The more you understand the outer—not merely the fact of the distance between here and the moon, technological knowledge, but the outward movements of society, of nations, the wars, the hate that there is—when you understand the outer then you can go very deeply inwardly and that inward depth has no limit. You do not say, "I have reached the end, this is enlightenment." Enlightenment cannot be given by another; enlightenment comes when there is the understanding of confusion; and to understand confusion one must look at it.

Questioner: If you say that the thinker and the thought are not separate; and that if one thinks that the thinker is separate and thereby tries to control thought, that that merely brings back the struggle and the complexity of the mind; that there cannot be stillness that way, then I do not understand—if the thinker is the thought—how the separation arises in the first place. How can thought fight against itself?

Krishnamurti: How does the separation between the thinker and the thought arise when they are actually one? Is that so with you? Is it actually a fact that the thinker is the thought—or do you think it should be that way, therefore it is not an actuality for you? To realize that, you have to have great energy; that is to say, when you see a tree you have to have the energy not to have this division as "me" and the tree. To realize that, you need tremendous energy; then there is no division and therefore no conflict between the two; there is no control. But as most of us are conditioned to this idea, that the thinker is different from thought—then the conflict arises.

Questioner: Why do we find ourselves so difficult?

Krishnamurti: Because we have very complex minds—have we not? We are not simple people who look at things simply; we have complex minds. And society evolves, becoming more and more complex—like our own minds. To understand something very complex one has to be very simple. To understand something complex, a very complex problem, you must look at the problem itself without bringing into the investigation all the conclusions, answers, suppositions and theories. When you look at the problem —and knowing that the answer is in the problem—your mind becomes very simple; the simplicity is in the observation, not in the problem which may be complex.

Questioner: How can I see the whole thing, everything, as whole?

Krishnamurti: One is used to looking at things fragmentarily, seeing the tree as something separate, the wife as separate, the office, the boss—everything in fragments. How can I see the world, of which I am a part, completely, totally, not in divisions? Now, just listen, Sir, just listen: who is going to answer that question? Who is going to tell you how to look—the speaker? You have put the question and you are waiting for an answer—from whom? If the question is really very serious—I am not saying your question is wrong—if the question is really serious, then what is the problem? The problem then is: "I can't see things totally, because I look at everything in fragments!" When does the mind look at things in fragments? Why? Love my wife and hate my boss!—You understand? If I love my wife I must also love everybody. No? Don't say yes, because you do not; you do not love your wife and children, you do not, although you may talk about it. If you love your wife and children, you will educate them differently, you will care, not financially, but in a different way. Only when there is love, is there no division. You understand, Sir? When you hate there is division, then you are anxious, greedy, envious, brutal, violent; but when you love—not love with your mind, love is not a word, love is not pleasure—when you really love, then pleasure, sex and so on have quite a different quality; in that love there is no division. Division arises when there is fear. When you love there is no "me" and "you," "we" and "they." But now you will say, "How am I to love? How am I to get that perfume?" There is only one answer to that; look at yourself, observe yourself; do not beat yourself, but observe, and out of this observation, seeing things as they are, then, perhaps you will have that love. But one has to work very hard at observation, not being lazy, not being inattentive.

London, March 23, 1969

PART II

4. Can Man Change?

Energy. Its wastage in conflict.

We look at conditions prevailing in the world and observe what is happening there—the students' riots, the class prejudices, the conflict of black against white, the wars, the political confusion, the divisions caused by nationalities and religions. We are also aware of conflict, struggle, anxiety, loneliness, despair, lack of love, and fear. Why do we accept all this? Why do we accept the moral, social environment knowing very well that it is utterly immoral; knowing this for ourselves—not merely emotionally or sentimentally but looking at the world and at ourselves— why do we live this way? Why is it that our educational system does not turn out real human beings but mechanical entities trained to accept certain jobs and finally die? Education, science and religion have not solved our problems at all.

Looking at all this confusion, why does each one of us accept and conform, instead of shattering the whole process in ourselves? I think we should ask this question, not intellectually, nor in order to find some god, some realization, some peculiar happiness which inevitably leads to escapes of various kinds, but looking at it quietly, with steady eyes, without any judgment and evaluation. We should ask, as grown-up people, why it is that we live this way—live, struggle and die. And when we do ask such a question seriously, with full intention to understand it, philosophies, theories, speculative ideations have no place at all. What matters is not what should be or what might be or what principle we should follow, what kind of ideals we should have or to what religion or to which guru we should turn. All those responses are obviously utterly meaningless when you are confronted with this confusion, with the misery and constant conflict in which we live. We have made life into a battlefield, each family, each group, each nation against the other. Seeing all this, not as an idea, but as something which you actually observe, are confronted with, you will ask yourself what it is all about. Why do we go on in this way, neither living nor loving, but full of fear and terror till we die?

When you ask this question, what will you do? It cannot be asked by those people who are comfortably settled in familiar ideals, in a comfortable house, with a little money and who are highly respectable, bourgeois. If they do ask questions, such people translate them according to their individual demands for satisfaction. But as this is a very human, ordinary problem, which touches the life of every one of us, rich and poor, young and old, why do we live this monotonous, meaningless life, going to the office or working in a laboratory or a factory for forty years, breeding a few children, educating them in absurd ways, and then dying? I think you should ask this question with all your being, in order to find out. Then you can ask the next question: whether human beings can ever change radically, fundamentally, so that they look at the world anew with different eyes, with a different heart, no longer filled with hatred, antagonism, racial prejudices, but with a mind that is very clear, that has tremendous energy.

Seeing all this—the wars, the absurd divisions which religions have brought about, the separation between the individual and the community, the family opposed to the rest of the world, each human being clinging to some peculiar ideal, dividing himself into "me" and "you," "we" and "they"—seeing all this, both objectively and psychologically, there remains only one question, one fundamental problem and this is whether the human mind, which is so heavily conditioned, can change. Not in some future incarnation, nor at the end of life, but change radically now, so that the mind becomes new, fresh, young, innocent, unburdened, so that we know what it means to love and to live in peace. I think this is the only problem. When this is solved, every other problem, economic or social, all those things which lead to wars will end, and there will be a different structure of society.

So our question is, whether the mind, the brain and the heart can live as though for the first time, uncontaminated, fresh, innocent, knowing what it means to live happily, ecstatically with deep love. You know, there is danger in listening to rhetorical questions; this is not a rhetorical question at all—it is our life. We are not concerned with words or with ideas. Most of us are caught up with words, never realizing deeply that the word is never the thing, the description is never the thing described. And if we could, during these talks, try to understand this deep problem, how the human mind—involving as it does the brain, the mind and the heart—has been conditioned through centuries, by propaganda, fear and other influences, then we could ask whether that mind can undergo a radical transformation; so that men can live peacefully throughout the world, with great love, with great ecstasy and the realization of that which is immeasurable.

This is our problem, whether the mind, which is so burdened with past memories and traditions, can without effort, struggle or conflict, bring about the flame of change within itself and burn away the dross of yesterday. Having put that question—which I am sure every thoughtful, serious person asks—where shall we begin? Shall we begin with change in the bureaucratic world, in the social structure, outwardly? Or shall we start inwardly, that is psychologically? Shall we consider the outside world, with all its technological knowledge, the marvels of what man has done in the scientific field, shall we begin there and bring about a revolution? Man has tried that, too. He has said, when you change the outer things radically, as all the bloody revolutions of history have done, then man will change and he will be a happy human being. The Communist and other revolutions have said: bring about order outside and there will be order within. They have also said that it doesn't matter if there is no order within, what matters is that we should have order in the world outside —ideational order, a Utopia, in the name of which millions have been killed.

So let us begin inwardly, psychologically. This doesn't mean that you let the present social order, with all its confusion and disorder, remain as it is. But is there a division between inner and outer? Or is there only one movement in which the inner and the outer exist, not as two separate things but simply as movement? I think it is very important, if we are to establish not only verbal communication—speaking English as our common language, using words that we both understand—also to make use of a different kind of communication; because we are going to go into things very deeply and very seriously, so there must be communication within and beyond verbal communication. There must be communion, which implies that both of us are profoundly concerned, care, and look at this problem with affection, with an urge to understand it. So there must be not only verbal communication, but also a deep communion in which there is no question of agreement or disagreement. Agreement and disagreement should never arise, because we are not dealing with ideas, opinions, concepts or ideals—we are concerned with the problem of human change. And neither your opinion nor my opinion has any value at all. If you say that it is impossible to change human beings, who have been like this for thousands of years, you have already blocked yourself, you will not proceed, you will not begin to inquire or to explore. Or if you merely say that this is possible, then you live in a world of possibilities, not of realities.

So one must come to this question without saying it is

or it is not possible to change. One must come to it with a fresh mind, eager to find out, young enough to examine and explore. We must not only establish clear, verbal communication, but there should be communion between the speaker and yourself, a feeling of friendship and affection which exists when we are all tremendously concerned about something. When husband and wife are deeply concerned about their children, they put aside all opinions, their particular likes and dislikes, because they are concerned about the child. In that concern there is great affection, it is not an opinion that controls action. Similarly there must be that feeling of deep communion between you and the speaker, so that we are both faced with the same problem with the same intensity at the same time. Then we can establish this communion which alone brings about a deep understanding.

So there is this question as to how the mind, deeply conditioned as it is, can change radically. I hope you are putting this question to yourself, because unless there is morality which is not social morality, unless there is austerity which is not the austerity of the priest with his harshness and violence, unless there is order deeply within, this search for truth, for reality, for God—or for whatever name you like to give it—has no meaning at all. Perhaps those of you who have come here to find out how to realize God or how to have some mysterious experience, will be disappointed; because unless you have a new mind, a fresh mind, eyes that see what is true, you cannot possibly understand the immeasurable, the nameless, that which *is*.

If you merely want wider, deeper experiences but lead a shoddy, meaningless life, then you will have experiences that won't be worth anything. We must go into this together—you will find this question very complex because many things are involved in it. To understand it there must be freedom and energy; those two things we must all have—great energy and freedom to observe. If you are tied to a particular belief, if you are tethered to a particular ideational Utopia, obviously you are not free to look.

There is this complex mind, conditioned as Catholic or Protestant, looking for security, bound by ambition and tradition. For a mind that has become shallow—except in the technological field—going to the moon is a marvelous achievement. But those who built the spacecraft lead their own shoddy lives, petty, jealous, anxious and ambitious and their minds are conditioned. We are asking whether such minds can be completely free from all conditioning, so that a totally different kind of life can be lived. To find this out, there must be freedom to observe, not as a Christian, a Hindu, a Dutchman, a German, or a Russian or as anything else. To observe very clearly there must be freedom, which implies that the very observation is action. That very observation brings about a radical revolution. To be capable of such observation, you need great energy.

So we are going to find out why human beings do not have the energy, the drive, the intensity to change. They have any amount of energy to quarrel, to kill each other, to divide the world, to go to the moon—they have got energy for these things. But apparently they have not the energy to change themselves radically. So we are asking why haven't we this necessary energy?

I wonder what your response is when such a question is put to you? We said, man has enough energy to hate; when there is a war he fights, and when he wants to escape from what really is, he has the energy to run away from it—through ideas, through amusements, through gods, through drink. When he wants pleasure, sexual or otherwise, he pursues these things with great energy. He has the intelligence to overcome his environment, he has the energy to live at the bottom of the sea or to live in the skies—for this he has got vital energy. But apparently he has not the energy to change even the smallest habit. Why? Because we dissipate that energy in conflict within ourselves. We are not trying to persuade you of anything, we are not making propaganda, we are not replacing old ideas with new ones. We are trying to discover, to understand.

You see, we realize that we must change. Let us take as an example violence and brutality—those are facts. Human beings are brutal and violent; they have built a society which is violent in spite of all that the religions have said about loving your neighbor and loving God. All these things are just ideas, they have no value whatsoever, because man remains brutal, violent, and selfish. And being violent, he invents the opposite, which is nonviolence. Please go into this with me.

Man is trying all the time to become nonviolent. So there is conflict between what is, which is violence, and what should be, which is nonviolence. There is conflict between the two. That is the very essence of wastage of energy. As long as there is duality between what is and what should be—man trying to become something else, making an effort to achieve what "should be"—that conflict is waste of energy. As long as there is conflict between the opposites, man has not enough energy to change. Why should I have the opposite at all, as nonviolence, as the ideal? The ideal is not real, it has no meaning, it only leads to various forms of hypocrisy; being violent and pretending not to be violent. Or if you say you are an idealist and will eventually become peaceful, that is a great pretense, an excuse, because it will take many years for you to be without violence—indeed it may never happen. In the meantime you are a hypocrite and still violent. So if we can, not in abstraction but actually, put aside completely all ideals and only deal with the fact—which is violence— then there is no wastage of energy. This is really very important to understand, it isn't a particular theory of the speaker. As long as man lives in the corridor of opposites he must waste energy and therefore he can never change.

So with one breath you could wipe away all ideologies, all opposites. Please go into it and understand this; it is really quite extraordinary what takes place. If a man who

49

is angry pretends or tries not to be angry, in that there is conflict. But if he says, "I will observe what anger is, not try to escape or rationalize it," then there is energy to understand and put an end to anger. If we merely develop an idea that the mind must be free from conditioning, there will remain a duality between the fact and what "should be." Therefore it is a waste of energy. Whereas if you say, "I will find out in what manner the mind is conditioned," it is like going to the surgeon when one has cancer. The surgeon is concerned with operating and removing the disease. But if the patient is thinking about what a marvelous time he is going to have afterward, or is frightened about the operation, that is waste of energy.

We are concerned only with the fact that the mind is conditioned and not that the mind "should be free." If the mind is unconditioned it *is* free. So we are going to find out, examine very closely, what makes the mind so conditioned, what are the influences that have brought about this conditioning, and why we accept it. First of all, tradition plays an enormous part in life. In that tradition the brain has developed so that it can find physical security. One cannot live without security, that is the very first, primary animal demand, that there be physical security; one must have a house, food, and clothing. But the psychological way in which we use this necessity for security brings about chaos within and without. The psyche, which is the very structure of thought, also wants to be secure inwardly, in all its relationships. Then the trouble begins. There must be physical security for everybody, not only for the few; but that physical security for everybody is denied when psychological security is sought through nations, through religions, through the family. I hope you understand and that we have established some kind of communication between us.

So there is the necessary conditioning for physical security, but when there is the search and the demand for psychological security, then conditioning becomes tremendously potent. That is, psychologically, in our relationship with ideas, people, and things, we want security, but is there security at all, in any relationship? Obviously there is not. Wanting security psychologically is to deny outward security. If I want to be secure psychologically as a Hindu, with all the traditions, superstitions and ideas, I identify myself with the larger unit which gives me great comfort. So I worship the flag, the nation, the tribe and separate myself from the rest of the world. And this division obviously brings about insecurity physically. When I worship the nation, the customs, the religious dogmas, the superstitions, I separate myself within these categories and then obviously I must deny physical security for everybody else. The mind needs physical security, which is denied when it seeks psychological security. This is a fact, not an opinion—it is so. When I seek security in my family, my wife, my children, my house, I must be against the world, I must separate myself from other families, be against the rest of the world.

One can see very clearly how the conditioning begins, how two thousand years of propaganda in the Christian world has made it worship its culture, while the same kind of thing has been going on in the East. So the mind through propaganda, through tradition, through the desire to be secure, begins to condition itself. But is there any security psychologically, in relationship with ideas, with people and with things?

If relationship means being in contact with things directly, you are unrelated if you are not in contact. If I have an idea, an image about my wife, I am not related to her. I may sleep with her but I am not related to her, because my image of her prevents my directly coming into contact with her. And she, with her image, prevents a direct relationship with me. Is there any psychological certainty or security such as the mind is always seeking? Obviously when you observe any relationship very closely, there is no certainty. In the case of husband and wife or boy and girl who want to etstablish a firm relationship, what happens? When the wife or the husband looks at anyone else there is fear, jealousy, anxiety, anger, and hatred; there is no permanent relationship. Yet the mind all the time wants the feeling of belonging.

So that is the factor of conditioning, through propaganda, newspapers, magazines, from the pulpit, and one becomes tremendously aware how necessary it is not to rely on outside influences at all. You then find out what it means not to be influenced. Please follow this. When you read a newspaper you are influenced, consciously or unconsciously. When you read a novel or a book you are influenced; there is pressure, strain, to put what you read into some category. That is the whole purpose of propaganda. It begins at school and you go through life repeating what others have said. You are therefore secondhand human beings. How can such a secondhand human being find out something that is original, that is true? It is very important to understand what conditioning is and to go into this very deeply; as you look at it you have the energy to break down all those conditionings that hold the mind.

Perhaps now you would like to ask questions and so go into this matter, bearing in mind that it is very easy to ask questions, but to ask the right question is one of the most difficult things. Which doesn't mean the speaker is preventing you from asking questions. We must ask questions, we must doubt everything anybody has said, books, religions, authorities, everything! We must question, doubt, be skeptical. But we must also know when to let skepticism go by and to ask the right question, because in that very question lies the answer. So if you want to ask questions, please do.

Questioner: Sir, are you crazy?

Krishnamurti: Are you asking the speaker if he is crazy? Good. I wonder what you mean by that word "crazy"; do you mean unbalanced, mentally ill, with peculiar ideas, neurotic? All these are implied in that word "crazy." Who is the judge—you or I or somebody else? Seriously, who is the judge? Will the crazy person judge who is crazy and who is not crazy? If you judge whether the speaker is balanced or unbalanced, is not judgment part of the craziness of this world? To judge somebody, not knowing a thing about him except his reputation, the image that you have about him. If you judge according to the reputation and the propaganda which you have swallowed, then are you capable of judging? Judgment implies vanity; whether the judge be neurotic or sane, there is always vanity. Can vanity perceive what is true?—or do you not need great humility to look, to understand, to love? Sir, it's one of the most difficult things to be sane in this abnormal, insane world. Sanity implies having no illusion, no image at all about oneself or about another. You say, "I am this, I am that, I am great, I am small, I am good, I am noble"; all those epithets are images about oneself. When one has an image about oneself one is surely insane, one lives in a world of illusion. And I am afraid most of us do. When you call yourself a Dutchman—forgive me for saying so—you are not quite balanced. You separate yourself, isolate yourself—as others do when they call themselves Hindus. These nationalistic, religious divisions, with their armies, with their priests, indicate a state of mental insanity.

Questioner: Can you understand violence without having the opposite of it?

Krishnamurti: When the mind wants to stay with violence it invites the ideal of nonviolence. Look, that is very simple. I want to remain with violence, which is what I am, what human beings are—brutal. But I have the tradition of ten thousand years which says, "Cultivate nonviolence." So there is the fact that I am violent and thought says, "Look, you must be nonviolent." That is my conditioning. How am I to be free of my conditioning so that I look, so that I remain with violence and understand it, go through

53

it and finish with it?—not only at the superficial level but also deep down, at the so-called unconscious level. How is the mind not to be caught in the ideal? Is that the question?

Please listen. We are not talking about Martin Luther King or Mr. Gandhi, or X, Y, Z. We are not concerned with these people at all—they have their ideals, their conditioning, their political ambitions, and I am not concerned with any of that. We are dealing with what *we* are, you and I, the human beings we are. As human beings we are violent, we are conditioned through tradition, propaganda, culture, to create the opposite; we use the opposite when it suits us and we don't use it if it doesn't suit us. We use it politically or spiritually in different ways. But what we are now saying is that when the mind wants to stay with violence and understand it completely, tradition and habit come in and interfere. They say, "You must have the ideal of nonviolence." There is the fact and there is the tradition. How is the mind to break away from the tradition in order to give all this attention to violence? That is the question. Have you understood it? There is the fact that I am violent, and there is the tradition which says I must not be. Now I will look, not at violence, but at the tradition only. If it interferes with my wanting to pay attention to violence, why does it interfere? Why does it come in? My concern is not understanding violence, but understanding the interference of tradition. Have you got it? I give my attention to *that,* and then it doesn't interfere. So I find out why tradition plays such an important part in one's life—tradition being habit. Whether it is the habit of smoking, or drinking, a sexual habit or habit of speech—why do we live in habits? Are we aware of them? Are we aware of our traditions? If you are not completely aware, if you do not understand the tradition, the habit, the routine, then it is bound to impinge, to interfere with what you want to look at. It is one of the easiest things to live in habits, but to break this down implies a great many things—I may lose my job. When I try to break through I am afraid, because to live in habit gives me security, makes me feel certain, because all other human beings are doing the same. To stand up in a Dutch world suddenly and say "I am not a Dutchman" produces a shock. So there is fear. And if you say "I am against this whole established order, which is disorder," you'll be thrown out; so you are afraid, and you accept. Tradition plays an extraordinarily important part in life. Have you ever tried to eat a meal to which you are not accustomed? Find out and you will see how your stomach and your tongue will rebel. If you are in the habit of smoking you go on smoking, and to break the habit you'll spend years fighting it.

So the mind finds security in habits, saying, "My family, my children, my house, my furniture." When you say "my furniture" you *are* that furniture. You may laugh, but when that particular furniture which you love is taken away from you, you get angry. You are that furniture, that house, that money, that flag. To live in that way is to live not only a shallow, stupid life, but to live in routine and boredom. And when you live in routine and boredom you must have violence.

Amsterdam, May 3, 1969

5. Why Can't We Live at Peace?

**Fear, how it arises.
Time and thought.
Attention: to keep "awake."**

It seems strange that we cannot find a way of living in which there is neither conflict, nor misery, nor confusion but a great abundance of love and consideration. We read books by intellectual people which tell us how society should be organized economically, socially and morally. Then we turn to books by religious people and theologians with their speculative ideas. Apparently it seems very difficult for most of us to find a way of living which is alive, peaceful, full of energy and clarity, without depending on others. We are supposed to be very mature and sophisticated people. Those of us who are older have lived through two appalling wars, through revolutions, upheavals, and every form of unhappiness. And yet here we are, on a beautiful morning, talking about all these things, perhaps waiting to be told what to do, to be shown a practical way of living, to follow somebody who may give us some key to the beauty of life and the greatness of something beyond the daily round.

I wonder—and so may you—why we listen to others. Why is it that we cannot find clarity for ourselves in our own minds and hearts, without any distortion; why need we be burdened by books? Can we not live unperturbed, fully, with great ecstasy and really at peace? This state of affairs seems to me very odd indeed, but there it is. Have you ever wondered if you could live a life completely without any effort or strife? We are endlessly making effort to change this, to transform that, to suppress this, to accept that, to imitate, to follow certain formulas and ideas.

And I wonder if we have ever asked ourselves if it is possible to live without conflict—not in intellectual isolation or in an emotional, sentimental, rather woolly way of life—but to live without any kind of effort at all. Because effort, however pleasant (or unpleasant), gratifying or profitable, does distort and pervert the mind. It is like a machine that is always grinding, never running smoothly and so wearing itself out very quickly. Then one asks—and I think it is a worthwhile question—whether it is possible to live without effort, but without becoming lazy, isolated, indifferent, lacking in sensitivity, without becoming a sluggish human being. All our life, from the moment we are born till we die, is an endless struggle to adjust, to change, to become something. And this struggle and conflict make for confusion, dull the mind and our hearts become insensitive.

So is it possible—not as an idea, or as something hopeless, beyond our measure—to find a way to live without conflict, not merely superficially but also deep down in the so-called unconscious, within our own depths? Perhaps this morning we can go into that question very deeply.

First of all, why do we invent conflicts, either pleasurable or unpleasurable, and is it possible to end this? Can we end this and live a totally different kind of life, with great energy, clarity, intellectual capacity, reason, and have a heart that is full of abundant love in the real sense of the word? I think we should apply our minds and our hearts to find out, get involved in this completely.

There is obviously conflict because of contradiction in ourselves, which expresses itself outwardly in society, in the activity of the "me" and the "not me." That is, the "me" with all its ambitions, drives, pursuits, pleasure, anxieties, hate, competition, and fears, and the "other" which is "not me." There is also the idea about living without conflict or opposing contradictory desires, pursuits, and drives. If we are aware of this tension, we can see this in ourselves, the pulls of contradictory demands, opposing beliefs, ideas, and pursuits.

It is this duality, these opposing desires with the fears and contradictions that bring about conflict. I think that is fairly clear, if we watch it in ourselves. The pattern of it is repeated over and over again, not only in daily life but also in so-called religious living—between heaven and hell, the good and the bad, the noble and ignoble, love and hate, and so on. If I may suggest, please do not merely listen to the words but observe yourselves nonanalytically, using the speaker as a mirror in which you see yourselves factually, so that you become aware of the workings of your own mind and heart, as you look into that mirror. One can see how any form of division, separation or contradiction, within or outside oneself, inevitably brings conflict between violence and nonviolence. Realizing this state of affairs as it is actually, is it possible to end it, not only at the superficial level of our consciousness, in our daily living, but also deep down at the very roots of our being, so that there is no contradiction, no opposing demands and desires, no activity of the dualistic fragmentary mind? Now how is this to be done? One builds a bridge between the "me" and the "not me"—the "me" with all its ambitions, drives, and contradictions, and the "not me" which is the ideal, which is the formula, the concept. We are always trying to build a bridge between "what is" and "what should be." And in that there is contradiction and conflict and all our energies are wasted in this way. Can the mind stop dividing and remain entirely with what *is?* In the understanding of what is, is there any conflict at all?

I would like to go into this question, looking at it differently, in relation to freedom and fear. Most of us want freedom, though we live in self-centered activity and our days are spent in concern about ourselves, our failures and fulfillments. We want to be free—not only politically, which is comparatively easy, except in the world of dictatorships—but also free from religious propaganda. Any religions, ancient or modern, is the work of propagandists and is therefore not religion at all. The more serious one is, the more one is concerned with the whole business of living, the more one seeks freedom and is questioning, without accepting or believing. One wants to be free in order to find out whether there is such a thing as reality, whether there is something eternal, timeless, or not. There is this extraordinary demand to be free in every relationship, but that freedom generally becomes a self-isolating process and therefore is not true freedom.

In the very demand for freedom there is fear. Because freedom may involve complete, absolute insecurity and one is frightened of being completely insecure. Insecurity seems a very dangerous thing—every child demands security in its relationships. And as we grow older we keep on demanding security and certainty in all relationships—with things, with people, and with ideas. That demand for security inevitably breeds fear and being afraid we depend more and more on the things to which we are attached. So there arises this question of freedom and fear and whether it is at all possible to be free of fear; not only physically, but psychologically, not only superficially but deep down in the dark corners of our mind, in the very secret recesses into which no penetration has been made. Can the mind be utterly, completely free from all fear? It is fear that destroys love—this is not a theory—it is fear that makes for anxiety, attachment, possessiveness, domination, jealousy in all relationships, it is fear that makes for violence. As one can observe in the overcrowded cities with their exploding populations, there is great insecurity, uncertainty, fear. And it is partly this that makes for violence. Can we be free of fear, so that when you leave this hall you walk out without any shadow of the darkness that fear brings?

To understand fear we must examine not only physical fears but the vast network of psychological fears. Perhaps we can go into this. The question is: how does fear arise —what keeps it sustained, gives it duration, and is it possible to end it? Physical fears are fairly easy to understand. There is instant response to physical danger and that response is the response of many centuries of conditioning, because without this there would not have been physical survival, life would have ended. Physically one must survive and the tradition of thousands of years says "be careful," memory says "be careful there is danger, act immediately." But is this physical response to danger fear?

Please do follow all this carefully, because we are going to go into something quite simple, yet complex, and unless you give your whole attention to it we shall not understand it. We are asking whether that physical, sensory response to danger involving immediate action is fear? Or is it intelligence and therefore not fear at all? And is intelligence a matter of the cultivation of tradition and memory? If it is, why doesn't it operate completely, as it should, in the psychological field, where one is so terribly frightened about so many things? Why doesn't that same intelligence which we find when we observe danger, operate when there are psychological fears? Is this physical intelligence applicable to the psychological nature of man? That is, there are fears of various kinds which we all know —fear of death, of darkness, what the wife or the husband will say or do, or what the neighbor or the boss will think —the whole network of fears. We are not going to deal with the details of various forms of fear; we are concerned with fear itself, not a particular fear. And when there is fear and we become aware of it, there is a movement to escape from it; either suppressing it, running away from it, or taking flight through various forms of entertainment, including religious ones, or developing courage which is resistance to fear. Escape, entertainment, and courage are all various forms of resistance to the actual fact of fear.

The greater the fear the greater the resistance to it and so various neurotic activities are set up. There is fear, and the mind—or the "me"—says "there must be no fear," and so there is duality. There is the "me" which is different from fear, which escapes from fear and resists it, which cultivates energy, theorizes or goes to the analyst; and there is the "not me!" The "not me" is fear; the "me" is separate from that fear. So there is immediate conflict between the fear, and the "me" that is overcoming that fear. There is the watcher and the watched. The watched being fear, and the watcher being the "me" that wants to get rid of that fear. So there is an opposition, a contradiction, a separation and hence there is conflict between fear and the "me" that wants to be rid of that fear. Are we communicating with each other?

So the problem consists of this conflict between the "not me" of fear and the "me" who thinks it is different from it and resists fear; or who tries to overcome it, escape from it, suppress it or control it. This division will invariably bring conflict, as it does between two nations with their armies and their navies and their separate sovereign governments.

So there is the watcher and the thing watched—the watcher saying "I must get rid of this terrible thing, I must do away with it." The watcher is always fighting, is in a state of conflict. This has become our habit, our tradition, our conditioning. And it is one of the most difficult things to break any kind of habit, because we like to live in habits, such as smoking, drinking, or sexual or psychological habits; and so it is with nations, sovereign governments which say "my country and your country," "my God and your God," "my belief and your belief." It is our tradition to fight, to resist fear and therefore increase the conflict and so give more life to fear.

If this is clear, then we can go on to the next step, which is: is there any actual difference between the watcher and the watched, in this particular case? The watcher thinks he is different from the watched, which is fear. Is there any difference between him and the thing he watches or are they both the same? Obviously they are both the same. The watcher is the watched—if something totally new comes along then there is no watcher at all. But because the watcher recognizes his reaction as fear, which he has known previously, there is this division. And as you go into it very, very deeply, you discover for yourself—as I hope you are doing now—that the watcher and the watched are essentially the same. Therefore if they are the same, you eliminate altogether the contradiction, the "me" and the "not me," and with them you also wipe away all kinds of effort totally. But this does not mean that you accept fear, or identify yourself with fear.

There is fear, the thing watched, and the watcher who is part of that fear. So what is to be done? (Are you working as hard as the speaker is working? If you merely listen to the words, then I am afraid you will not solve this question of fear deeply.) There is only fear—not the watcher who watches fear, because the watcher *is* fear. There are several things that take place. First, what is fear and how does it come about? We are not talking about the results of fear, or the cause of fear, or how it darkens one's life with its misery and ugliness. But we are asking what fear is and how it comes about. Must one analyze it continuously to discover the endless causes of fear? Because when you begin to analyze, the analyzer must be extraordinarily free from all prejudices and conditionings; he has to look, to observe. Otherwise if there is any kind of distortion in his judgment, that distortion increases as he continues to analyze.

So analysis in order to end fear is not the ending of it. I hope there are some analysts here! Because in discovering the cause of fear and acting upon that discovery, the cause becomes the effect, and the effect becomes the cause. The effect, and acting upon that effect in order to find the cause, and discovering the cause and acting according to that cause, becomes the next stage. It becomes both effect and cause in an endless chain. If we put aside the understanding of the cause of fear and the analysis of fear, then what is there to do?

You know, this is not an entertainment; but there is great joy in discovery, there is great fun in understanding all this. So what makes fear? Time and thought make fear—time as yesterday, today, and tomorrow; there is the fear that tomorrow something will happen—the loss of a job, death, that my wife or my husband will run away, that the disease and pain that I have had many days ago will come back again. This is where time comes in. Time involving what my neighbor may say about me tomorrow, or time which up to now has covered up something which I did many years ago. I am afraid of some deep secret desires which might not be fulfilled. So time is involved in fear, fear of death which comes at the end of life, which may be waiting around the corner and I am afraid. So time involves fear and thought. There is no time if there is no thought. Thinking about that which happened yesterday, being afraid that it may happen again tomorrow—this is what brings about time as well as fear.

Do watch this, please look at it for yourself—don't accept or reject anything; but listen, find out for yourself the truth of this, not just the words, not whether you agree or disagree, but go on. To find the truth you must have feeling, a passion for finding out, great energy. Then you will find that thought breeds fear; thinking about the past or the future—the future being the next minute or the next day or ten years hence—thinking about it makes it an event. And thinking about an event which was pleasurable yesterday, sustains or gives continuity to that pleasure, whether that pleasure be sexual, sensory, intellectual, or psychological; thinking about it, building an image as most people do, gives to that event in the past a continuity through thought and breeds more pleasure.

Thought breeds fear as well as pleasure; they are both matters of time. So thought engenders this two-sided coin of pleasure and pain—which is fear. Then what is there to do? We worship thought which has become so extraordinarily important that we think the more cunning it is, the better it is. In the business world, in the religious world, or in the world of the family, thought is used by the intellectual who indulges in the use of this coin, in the garland of words. How we honor the people who are intellectually, verbally clever in their thinking! But thinking is responsible for fear and the thing called pleasure.

We are not saying we shouldn't have pleasure. We are not being puritanical, we are trying to understand it, and in the very understanding of this whole process, fear comes to an end. Then you will see that pleasure is something entirely different, and we shall go into this if we have time. So thought is responsible for this agony—one side is agony, the other side is pleasure and its continuance: the demand for and the pursuit of pleasure, including the religious and every other form of pleasure. Then what is thought to do? Can it end? Is that the right question? And who is to end it?—is it the "me" who is not thought? But the "me" is the result of thought. And therefore you have again the same old problem; the "me" and the "not me" which is the watcher who says, "If only I could end thought then I'd live a different kind of life." But there is only thought and not the watcher who says, "I want to end thought," because the watcher is the product of thought. And how does thought come into being? One can see very easily, it is the response of memory, experience and knowledge which is the brain, the seat of memory. When anything is asked of it, it responds by a reaction which is memory and recognition. The brain is the result of millennia of evolution and conditioning—thought is always old, thought is never free, thought is the response of all conditioning.

What is to be done? When thought realizes that it cannot possibly do anything about fear because it creates fear, then there is silence; then there is complete negation of any movement which breeds fear. Therefore the mind, including the brain, observes this whole phenomenon of habit and the contradiction and struggle between the "me" and the "not me." It realizes that the watcher is the watched. And seeing that fear cannot be merely analyzed and put aside, but that it will always be there, the mind also sees that analysis is not the way. Then one asks: what is the origin of fear? How does it arise?

We said that it came about through time and thought. Thought is the response of memory and so thought creates fear. And fear cannot end through the mere control or suppression of thought, or by trying to transmute thought, or indulging in all the tricks one plays on oneself. Realizing this whole pattern choicelessly, objectively, in oneself, seeing all this, thought itself says, "I will be quiet without any control or suppression," "I will be still."

So then there is the ending of fear, which means the ending of sorrow and the understanding of oneself—self-knowing. Without knowing oneself there is no ending of sorrow and fear. It is only a mind that is free from fear that can face reality.

Perhaps you would now care to ask questions. One must ask questions—this asking, this exposing of oneself to oneself here is necessary, and also when you are by yourself in your room or in your garden, sitting quietly in the bus or walking—you must ask questions in order to find out. But one has to ask the right question, and in the very asking of the right question is the right answer.

Questioner: To accept oneself, one's pain, one's sorrow, is that the right thing to do?

Krishnamurti: How can one accept what one is? You mean to say you accept your ugliness, your brutality, your violence, your pretentiousness, your hypocrisies? Can you accept all that? And don't you want to change?—indeed musn't we change all this? How can we accept the established order of society with its morality which is immorality? Isn't life a constant movement of change? When one is living there is no acceptance, there is only living. We are then living with the movement of life and the movement of life demands change, psychological revolution, a mutation.

Questioner: I don't understand.

Krishnamurti: I'm sorry. Perhaps when you used the word "accept" you did not realize that in ordinary English that means to accept things as they are. Perhaps you would put it in Dutch.

Questioner: Accept things as they come.

Krishnamurti: Will I accept things as they come, say, when my wife leaves me? When I lose money, when I lose my job, when I am despised, insulted, will I accept these things as they come? Will I accept war? To take things as they come, actually, not theoretically, one must be free of the "me," the "I." And that is what we have been talking about this morning, the emptying of the mind of the "me" and "you," and the "we" and "they." Then you can live from moment to moment, endlessly, without struggle, without conflict. But that is real meditation, real action, not conflict, brutality and violence.

Questioner: We have to think; it is inevitable.

Krishnamurti: Yes, I understand, Sir. Are you suggesting that we should not think at all? To do a job you have to think, to go to your house you have to think; there is the verbal communication, which is the result of thought. So what place has thought in life? Thought must operate when you are doing something. Please follow this. To do any technological job, to function as the computer does— even if not as efficiently—thought is needed. To think clearly, objectively, nonemotionally, without prejudice, without opinion; thought is necessary in order to act clearly. But we also know that thought breeds fear, and that very fear will prevent us from acting efficiently. So can one act without fear when thought is demanded, and be quiet when it is not? Do you understand? Can one have a mind and heart that understands this whole process of fear, pleasure, thought and the quietness of the mind? Can one act thoughtfully when it is necessary, and not use thought when it is not? Surely this is fairly simple, isn't it? That is, can the mind be so completely attentive that when it is awake it will think and act when necessary and remain awake in that action neither falling asleep nor working in a mechanical way?

So the question is not whether we must think or not, but how to keep awake. To keep awake one has to have this deep understanding of thought, fear, love, hate and loneliness; one has to be completely involved in this way of living *as one is* but understand completely. One can understand it deeply only when the mind is completely awake, without any distortion.

Questioner: Do you mean to say that in the face of danger you just react out of experience?

Krishnamurti: Don't you? When you see a dangerous animal, don't you react out of memory, out of experience?— perhaps not your personal experience but the racial inheritance which says "be careful."

Questioner: That is what I had in mind.

Krishnamurti: But why don't we act equally efficiently when we see the danger of nationalism, of war, of separate governments with their sovereign rights and armies? These are the most dangerous things; why don't we react, why don't we say, "Let's change all that"? This means that you change yourself—the known being; that you do not belong to any nation, to any flag, country or religion, so that you are a free human being. But we don't. We react to physical dangers but not to psychological dangers, which are much more devastating. We accept things as they are or we revolt against them to form some fanciful Utopia, which comes back to the same thing. To see danger inwardly and to see danger outwardly is the same thing, which is, to keep awake—which means to be intelligent and sensitive.

Amsterdam, May 10, 1969

6. The Wholeness of Life

The motiveless passion to understand.

One wonders why human beings throughout the world lack passion. They lust after power, position and various forms of entertainment both sexual and religious, and have other forms of lustful cravings. But apparently few have that deep passion which dedicates itself to the understanding of the whole process of living, not giving their whole energy to fragmentary activity. The bank manager is tremendously interested in his banking and the artist and the scientist are given over to their own special interests, but apparently it is one of the most difficult things to have an abiding, intense passion given over to the understanding of the wholeness of life.

As we go into this question of what constitutes the total understanding of living, loving and dying, we shall need not only intellectual capacity and strong feeling, but much more than these, great energy that only passion can give. As we have this enormous problem, complex, subtle and very profound, we must give our total attention—which is after all passion—to see and find out for ourselves if there is a way of life, wholly different from that which we now live. To understand this, one has to go into several questions, one has to inquire into the process of consciousness, examining both the surface and the deep layers of one's own mind, and one also has to look at the nature of order; not only outwardly, in society, but within oneself.

One has to find out the meaning of living, not merely giving an intellectual significance to it, but looking at what it means to live. And one has also to go into this question of what love is, and what it means to die. All this has to be examined in the conscious and the deep, hidden recesses of one's own mind. One has to ask what order is, what living really means, and whether one can live a life of complete, total affection, compassion, tenderness, and love. One has also to find out for oneself the meaning of that extraordinary thing called death.

These are not fragments, but the total movement, the wholeness of life. We shall not be able to understand this if we cut it up into living, loving, and dying—it is all one movement. To understand its total process, there must be energy, not only intellectual energy but energy of strong feeling, which involves having motiveless passion, so that it is constantly burning within one. And as our minds are fragmented, it is necessary to go into this question of the conscious and the unconscious, for *there* begins all division—the "me" and "not me," the "you" and "me," the "we" and "they." As long as this separation exists—nationally, in the family, between religions with their separate possessive dependencies—there will inevitably be divisions in life. There will be the living of everyday life with its boredom and routine and that thing which we call love, hedged about by jealousy, possessiveness, dependence, and domination, there will be fear, the inevitability of death. Could we go into this question seriously—not merely theoretically, or verbally, but really investigate it by looking into ourselves and asking why there is this division, which breeds so much misery, confusion, and conflict?

One can observe in oneself very clearly the activity of the superficial mind with its concern with livelihood, with its technological, scientific, acquisitive knowledge. One can see oneself being competitive in the office, one can see the superficial operations of one's own mind. But there are the hidden parts which have not been explored, because we don't know how to explore them. If we want to expose them to the light of clarity and understanding, we either read books which tell us all about it, or we go to some analyst or philosopher. But we do not know for ourselves how to look at things; though we may be capable of observing the outward, superficial activity of the mind, we are apparently incapable of looking into this deep, hidden cave in which the whole of the past abides. Can the conscious mind with its positive demands and assertions look into the deeper layers of one's own being? I do not know if you have ever tried it, but if you have and have been sufficiently insistent and serious, you may have found for yourself the vast content of the past, the racial inheritance, the religious impositions, the divisions; all these are hidden there. The casual offering of an opinion springs from that past accumulation, which is essentially based on past knowledge and experience, with their various forms of conclusions and opinions. Can the mind look into all this, understand it and go beyond it, so that there is no division at all?

This is important, because we are so conditioned to look at life in a fragmentary way. And as long as this fragmentation goes on, there is the demand for fulfillment—"me" wanting to fulfill, to achieve, to compete, to be ambitious. It is this fragmentation of life that makes us both individualistic and collective, self-centered yet needing to identify oneself with something greater, while remaining separate. It is this deep division in consciousness, in the whole structure and nature of our being that makes for division in our activities, in our thoughts and in our feelings. So we divide life and those things called loving and dying.

Is it possible to observe the movement of the past, which is the unconscious?—if one can use that word "unconscious" without giving it a special psychoanalytical significance. The deep unconscious is the past, and we are operating from that. Therefore there is the division into the past, the present and the future—which is time.

All this may sound rather complicated, but it is not—it is really quite simple if one can look into oneself, observe oneself in action, observe the workings of one's opinions and thoughts and conclusions. When you look at yourself critically you can see that your actions are based on a past conclusion, a formula or pattern, which projects itself into the future as an ideal and you act according to that ideal. So the past is always operating with its motives, conclusions, and formulas; the mind and the heart are heavily laden with memories, which are shaping our lives, bringing about fragmentation.

One must ask the question whether the conscious mind can see into the unconscious so completely that one has understood the whole of its content, which is the past. That demands a critical capacity—but not self-opinionated criticism—it demands that one should watch. If one is really awake, then this division in the totality of consciousness ends. That awakened state is possible only when there is this critical self-awareness devoid of judgment.

To observe means to be critical—not using criticism based on evaluation, on opinions, but to be critically watchful. But if that criticism is personal, hedged by fear or any form of prejudice, it ceases to be truly critical, it becomes merely fragmentary.

What we are now concerned with is the understanding of the total process, the wholeness of living, not with a particular fragment. We are not asking what to do with regard to a particular problem, with regard to social activity which is independent of the whole process of living; but we are trying to find out what is included in the understanding of reality and whether there is such a reality, such an immensity, eternity. It is this whole, total perception—not fragmentary perception—that we are concerned with. This understanding of the whole movement of life as one single unitary activity is possible only when in the whole of our consciousness there is the ending of one's own concepts, principles, ideas and divisions as the "me" and the "not me." If that is clear—and I hope it is —then we can proceed to find out what living is.

We consider living to be a positive action—doing, thinking, the everlasting bustle, conflict, fear, sorrow, guilt, ambition, competition, the lusting after pleasure with its pain, the desire to be successful. All this is what we call living. That is our life, with its occasional joy, with its moments of compassion without any motive, and generosity without any strings attached to it. There are rare moments of ecstasy, of a bliss that has no past or future. But going to the office, anger, hatred, contempt, enmity, are what we call everyday living, and we consider it extraordinarily positive.

The negation of the positive is the only true positive. To negate this so-called living, which is ugly, lonely, fearful, brutal, and violent, without knowledge of the other, is the most positive action. Are we communicating with each other? You know, to deny conventional morality completely is to be highly moral, because what we call social morality, the morality of respectability, is utterly immoral; we are competitive, greedy, envious, seeking our own way —you know how we behave. We call this social morality; religious people talk about a different kind of morality, but their life, their whole attitude, the hierarchical structure of religious organization and belief, is immoral. To deny that is not to react, because when you react, this is another form of dissenting through one's own resistance. But when you deny it because you understand it, there is the highest form of morality.

In the same way, to negate social morality, to negate the way we are living—our pretty little lives, our shallow thinking and existence, the satisfaction at a superficial level with our accumulated things—to deny all that, not as a reaction but seeing the utter stupidity and the destructive nature of this way of living—to negate all that is to live. To see the false as the false—this seeing is the true.

Then, what is love? Is love pleasure? Is love desire? Is

love attachment, dependence, possession of the person whom you love and dominate? Is it saying, "This is mine and not yours, my property, my sexual rights," in which are involved jeolousy, hate, anger, and violence? And again, love has been divided into sacred and profane as part of religious conditioning; is all that love? Can you love and be ambitious? Can you love your husband, can he say he loves you when he is ambitious? Can there be love when there is competition and the drive for success?

To negate all that, not only intellectually or verbally, but to wipe it out of one's own being, never to experience jealousy, envy, competition, or ambition—to deny all that, surely this is love. These two ways of acting cannot ever go together. The man who is jealous, or the woman who is dominating, doesn't know what love means—they may talk about it, they may sleep together, possess each other, depend on each other for comfort, security, or from fear of loneliness, but surely all that is not love. If people who say they love their children meant it, would there be war? And would there be division of nationalities—would there be these separations? What we call love is torture, despair, a feeling of guilt. This love is generally identified with sexual pleasure. We are not being puritanical or prudish, we are not saying that there must be no pleasure. When you look at a cloud or the sky or a beautiful face, there is delight. When you look at a flower there is the beauty of it—we are not denying beauty. Beauty is not the pleasure of thought, but it is thought that gives pleasure to beauty.

In the same way, when we love and there is sex, thought gives it pleasure, the image of that which has been experienced and the repetition of it tomorrow. In this repetition is pleasure which is not beauty. Beauty, tenderness and the total meaning of love don't exclude sex. But now when everything is allowed, the world suddenly seems to have discovered sex and it has become extraordinarily important. Probably that is the only escape man has now, the only freedom; everywhere else he is pushed around, bullied, violated intellectually, emotionally, in every way he is a slave, he is broken, and the only time when he can be free is in sexual experience. In that freedom he comes upon a certain joy and he wants the repetition of that joy. Looking at all this, where is love? Only a mind and a heart that are full of love can see the whole movement of life. Then whatever he does, a man who possesses such love is moral, good, and what he does is beautiful.

And where does order come into all this—knowing our life is so confused, so disorderly. We all want order, not only in the house, arranging things in their proper place, but we also want order externally, in society, where there is such immense social injustice. We also want order inwardly—there must be order, deep, mathematical order. And is this order to be brought about by conforming to a pattern which we consider to be orderly? Then we should be comparing the pattern with the fact, and there would be conflict. Is not this very conflict disorder?—and therefore not virtue. When a mind struggles to be virtuous, moral, ethical, it resists, and in that very conflict there is disorder. So virtue is the very essence of order—though we may not like to use that word in the modern world. That virtue is not brought about through the conflict of thought, but comes only when you see disorder critically, with wakened intelligence, understanding yourself. Then there is complete order of the highest form, which is virtue. And that can come only when there is love.

Then there is the question of dying, which we have carefully put far away from us, as something that is going to happen in the future—the future may be fifty years off or tomorrow. We are afraid of coming to an end, coming physically to an end and being separated from the things we have possessed, worked for, experienced—wife, husband, the house, the furniture, the little garden, the books and the poems we have written or hoped to write. And we are afraid to let all that go because we are the furniture, we are the picture that we possess; when we have the capacity to play the violin, we are that violin. Because we have identified ourselves with those things—we are all that and nothing else. Have you ever looked at it that way? You are the house—with the shutters, the bedroom, the furniture which you have very carefully polished for years, which you own—that is what you are. If you remove all that you are nothing.

And that is what you are afraid of—of being nothing. Isn't it very strange how you spend forty years going to the office and when you stop doing these things you have heart trouble and die? You are the office, the files, the manager or the clerk or whatever your position is; you are that and nothing else. And you have a lot of ideas about God, goodness, truth, what society should be—that is all. Therein lies sorrow. To realize for yourself that you are that is great sorrow, but the greatest sorrow is that you do not realize it. To see that and find out what it means, is to die.

Death is inevitable, all organisms must come to an end. But we are afraid to let the past go. We are the past, we are time, sorrow and despair, with an occasional perception of beauty, a flowering of goodness or deep tenderness as a passing, not an abiding thing. And being afraid of death, we say, "Shall I live again?"—which is to continue the battle, the conflict, the misery, owning things, the accumulated experience. The whole of the East believes in reincarnation. That which you are you would like to see reincarnated; but you are all this, this mess, this confusion, this disorder. Also, reincarnation implies that we shall be born to another life; therefore what you do now, today, matters, not how you are going to live when you are born into your next life—if there is such a thing. If you are going to be born again, what matters is how you live today, because today is going to sow the seed of beauty or the seed of sorrow. But those who believe so fervently in reincarnation do not know how to behave; if they were concerned with behavior, then they would not be concerned with tomorrow, for goodness is in the attention of today.

Dying is part of living. You cannot love without dying, dying to everything which is not love, dying to all ideals which are the projection of your own demands, dying to all the past, to the experience, so that you know what love means and therefore what living means. So living, loving, and dying are the same thing, which consists in living wholly, completely, now. Then there is action which is not contradictory, bringing with it pain and sorrow; there is living, loving, and dying in which there is action. That action is order. And if one lives that way—and one must, not in occasional moments but every day, every minute—then we shall have social order, then there will be the unity of man, and governments will be run on computers, not by politicians with their personal ambitions and conditioning. So to live is to love and to die.

Questioner: Can one be free instantly and live without conflicts or does it take time?

Krishnamurti: Can one live without the past immediately or does getting rid of the past take time? Does it take time to get rid of the past, and does this prevent one from living immediately? That is the question. The past is like a hidden cave, like a cellar where you keep your wine— if you have wine. Does it take time to be free of it? What is involved in taking time?—which is what we are used to. I say to myself, "I'll take time, virtue is a thing to be acquired, to be practiced day after day, I'll get rid of my hate, my violence, gradually, slowly"; that is what we are used to, that is our conditioning. And so we ask ourselves whether it is possible to throw away all the past gradually —which involves time. That is, being violent, I say, "I'll gradually get rid of this." What does that mean—"gradually," "step by step"? In the meantime I am being violent. The idea of getting rid of violence gradually is a form of hypocrisy. Obviously, if I am violent I can't get rid of it gradually, I must end it immediately. Can I end psychological things immediately? I cannot, if I accept the idea of gradually freeing myself from the past. But what matters is to see the fact as it is now, without any distortion. If I am jealous and envious, I must see this completely by total, not partial, observation. I look at my jealousy—why am I jealous? Because I am lonely, the person I depended upon left me, and I am suddenly faced with my emptiness, with my isolation and I am afraid of that, therefore I depend on you. And if you turn away I am angry, jealous. The fact is I am lonely, I need companionship, I need somebody not only to cook for me, to give me comfort, sexual pleasure and all the rest of it, but because basically I am alone. And that is why I am jealous. Can I understand this loneliness immediately? I can understand it only if I observe it, if I do not run away from it—if I can look at it, observe it critically, with awakened intelligence, not find excuses, try to fill the void or try to find a new companion. To look at this there must be freedom and when there is freedom to look I am free of jealousy. So the perception, the total observation of jealousy and the freedom from it, is not a matter of time, but of giving complete attention, critical awareness, observing choicelessly, instantly, all things as they arise. Then there is freedom—not in the future but now—from that which we call jealousy.

This applies equally to violence, anger, or any other habit, whether you smoke, drink, or have sexual habits. If we observe them very attentively, completely with our heart and mind, we are intelligently aware of their whole content; then there is freedom. Once this awareness is functioning, then whatever arises—anger, jealousy, violence, brutality, shades of double meaning, enmity, all these things can be observed instantly, completely. In that there is freedom, and the thing that was there ceases to be. So the past is not to be wiped away through time. Time is not the way to freedom. Is not this idea of gradualness a form of indolence, of incapacity to deal with the past instantly as it arises? When you have that astonishing capacity to observe clearly as it arises and when you give your mind and heart completely to observe it, then the past ceases. So time and thought do not end the past, for time and thought are the past.

Questioner: Is thought a movement of the mind? Is awareness the function of a motionless mind?

Krishnamurti: As we said the other day, thought is the response of memory, like a computer into which you have fed all kinds of information. And when you ask for the answer, what has been stored up in the computer responds. In this same way the mind, the brain, is the storehouse of the past, which is the memory, and when it is challenged it responds in thought according to its knowledge, experience, conditioning, and so on. So thought is the movement, or rather part of the movement, of the mind and the brain. The questioner wants to know whether awareness is a stillness of the mind. Can you observe anything—a tree, your wife, your neighbor, the politician, the priest, a beautiful face—without any movement of the mind? The images of your wife, of your husband, of your neighbor, the knowledge of the cloud or of pleasure, all that interferes, doesn't it? So when there is interference by an image of any kind, subtle or obvious, then there is no observation, there is no real, total awareness—there is only partial awareness. To observe clearly there must be no image coming in between the observer and the thing observed. When you look at a tree, can you look at it without the knowledge of that tree in botanical terms, or the knowledge of your pleasure or desire concerning it? Can you look at it so completely that the space between you—the observer—and the thing observed disappears? That doesn't mean that you become the tree! But when that space disappears, there is the cessation of the observer, and only the thing which is observed remains. In that observation there is perception, seeing the thing with extraordinary vitality, its color, its shape, the beauty of the leaf or trunk; when there is not the center of the "me" who is observing, you are intimately in contact with that which you observe.

There is movement of thought, which is part of the brain and the mind, when there is a challenge which must be answered by thought. But to discover something new, something that has never been looked at, there must be this intense attention without any movement. This is not something mysterious or occult which you have to practice for years and years; that is all sheer nonsense. It does take place when, between two thoughts, you are observing.

You know how the man discovered jet propulsion? How did it happen? He knew all there was to know about the combustion engine, and he was looking for some other method. To look, you must be silent—if you carry all the knowledge of your combustion engine with you, you'll find only that which you have learned. What you have learned must remain dormant, quiet—then you will discover something new. In the same way, in order to see your wife, your husband, the tree, the neighbor, the whole social structure which is disorder, you must silently find a new way of looking and therefore a new way of living and acting.

Questioner: How do we find the power to live without theories and ideals?

Krishnamurti: How do you have the power to live *with* them? How do you have this extraordinary energy to live with formulas, with ideals, with theories? You are living with those formulas—how do you have the energy? This energy is being dissipated in conflict. The ideal is over there and you are here, and you are trying to live according to that. So there is a division, there is conflict, which is waste of energy. So when you see the wastage of energy, when you see the absurdity of having ideals, formulas, concepts, all bringing about such constant conflict, when you see it, then you have the energy to live without it. Then you have abundance of energy, because then

80

there is no wastage through conflict at all. But you see, we are afraid to live that way, because of our conditioning. And we accept this structure of formulas and ideals, as others have done. We live with them, we accept conflict as the way of life. But when we see all this, not verbally, not theoretically, not intellectually, but feel with our whole being the absurdity of living that way, then we have the abundance of energy which comes when there is no conflict whatsoever. Then there is only the fact and nothing else. There is the fact that you are greedy, not the ideal that you should not be greedy—that is a waste of energy—but the fact you are greedy, possessive, and dominating. That is the only fact, and when you give your whole attention to that fact, then you have the energy to dissipate it and therefore you can live freely, without any ideal, without any principle, without any belief. And that is loving and dying to everything of the past.

Amsterdam, May 11, 1969

PART III

7. Fear

Resistance. Energy and attention.

Most of us are caught in habits—physical and psychological habits. Some of us are aware of them and others are not. If one is aware of these habits then is it possible to stop a particular habit instantly and not carry it on over many months and years? Being aware of one particular habit, is it possible to put an end to it without any form of struggle, to drop it instantly—the habit of smoking, the particular twitch of the head, the habitual smile or any one of the various peculiar habits one has? To become conscious of chattering endlessly about nothing, of the restlessness of the mind—can one do that without any form of resistance, or control, and thus end it easily without effort and immediately? In that are implied several things: first the understanding that struggle against something, like a particular habit, develops a form of resistance to that habit; and one learns that resistance in any form breeds more conflict. If one resists a habit, tries to suppress it, struggle against it, the very energy that is necessary to understand that habit is wasted in the struggle and control. In that is involved the second thing: one takes for granted that time is necessary, that any particular habit must be slowly worn out, must slowly be suppressed or got rid of.

We are accustomed on the one hand to the idea that it is only possible to be free of any habit through resistance, through developing the opposite habit, and on the other hand to the idea that we can only do it gradually over a period of time. But if one really examines it one sees that any form of resistance develops further conflicts and also that time, taking many days, weeks, years, does not really end the habit; and we are asking whether it is possible to end a habit without resistance and without time, immediately.

To be free of fear what is required is not resistance over a period of time but the energy that can meet this habit and dissolve it immediately: and that is attention. Attention is the very essence of all energy. To give one's attention means to give one's mind, one's heart, one's whole physical energy, to attend and with that energy to face, or to be aware of, the particular habit; then you will see that the habit has no longer any hold—it disappears instantly.

One may think that one's various habits are not particularly important—one has them, what does it matter; or one finds excuses for one's habits. But if one could establish the quality of attention in the mind, the mind having seized the fact, the truth, that energy is attention and that attention is necessary to dissolve any particular habit, then becoming aware of a particular habit, or tradition, one will see that it comes to an end, completely.

One has a way of talking or one indulges in endless chatter about nothing: if one becomes so attentively aware, then one has an extraordinary energy—energy that is not brought about through resistance, as most energies are. This energy of attention is freedom. If one understands this really very deeply, not as a theory but an actual fact with which one has experimented, a fact seen and of which one is fully aware, then one can proceed to inquire into the whole nature and structure of fear. And one must bear in mind, when talking about this rather complicated question, that verbal communication between you and the speaker becomes rather difficult; if one is not listening with sufficient care and attention then communication is not

83

possible. If you are thinking about one thing and the speaker is talking about something else, then communication comes to an end, obviously. If you are concerned with your own particular fear and your whole attention is given to that particular fear, then verbal communication between you and the speaker also comes to an end. To communicate with one another, verbally, there must be a quality of attention in which there is care, in which there is an intensity, an urgency to understand this question of fear.

More important than communication is communion. Communication is verbal and communion is nonverbal. Two people who know each other very well can, without saying any words, understand each other completely, immediately, because they have established a certain form of communication between themselves. When we are dealing with such a very complicated issue as fear, there must be communion as well as verbal communication; the two must go together all the time, or otherwise we shall not be working together. Having said all this—which is necessary—let us consider the question of fear.

It is not that you must be free *from* fear. The moment you try to free yourself from fear, you create a resistance against fear. Resistance, in any form, does not end fear—it will always be there, though you may try to escape from it, resist it, control it, run away from it and so on, it will always be there. The running away, the controlling, the suppressing, all are forms of resistance; and the fear continues even though you develop greater strength to resist. So we are not talking about being free from fear. Being free from something is not freedom. Please do understand this, because in going into this question, if you have given your whole attention to what is being said, you must leave this hall without any sense of fear. That is the only thing that matters, not what the speaker says or does not say or whether you agree or disagree; what is important is that one should totally, right through one's being, psychologically, end fear.

So, it is not that one must be free from or resist fear but that one must understand the whole nature and structure of fear, *understand it;* that means, learn about it, watch it, come directly into contact with it. We are to learn about fear, not how to escape from it, not how to resist it through courage and so on. We are to learn. What does that word mean, "to learn"? Surely it is not the accumulation of knowledge about fear. It will be rather useless going into this question unless you understand this completely. We think that learning implies the accumulation of knowledge about something; if one wants to learn Italian, one has to accumulate the words and their meaning, the grammar and how to put the sentences together and so on; having gathered knowledge then one is capable of speaking that particular language. That is, there is the accumulation of knowledge and then action; time is involved. Now, such accumulation we say is not learning. Learning is always in the active present, it is not the result of having accumulated knowledge; learning is a process, an action, which is always in the present. Most of us are accustomed to the idea of first of all accumulating knowledge, information, experience and from that acting. We are saying something entirely different. Knowledge is always in the past and when you act, the past is determining that acting. We are saying, learning is in the very action itself and therefore there is never an accumulation as knowledge.

Learning about fear is in the present, is something fresh. If I come upon fear with past knowledge, with past memories and associations, I do not come face to face with fear and therefore I do not learn about it. I can do this only if my mind is fresh, new. And that is our difficulty, because we always approach fear with all the associations, memories, incidents and experiences, all of which prevent us from looking at it afresh and learning about it anew.

There are many fears—fear of death, fear of darkness, fear of losing a job, fear of the husband or wife, insecurity, fear of not fulfilling, fear of not being loved, fear of loneliness, fear of not being a success. Are not these many fears the expression of one central fear? One asks, then: are we going to deal with a particular fear, or are we dealing with the fact of fear itself?

We want to understand the nature of fear, not how fear expresses itself in a particular direction. If we can deal with the central fact of fear, then we shall be able to resolve, or do something about, a particular fear. So do not take your particular fear and say, "I must resolve this," but understand the nature and structure of fear; then you will be able to deal with the particular fear.

See how important it is that the mind be in a state in which there is no fear whatsoever. Because when there is fear there is darkness and the mind becomes dull; then the mind seeks various escapes and stimulation through amusement—whether the amusement be in the Church or on the football field or on the radio. Such a mind is afraid, is incapable of clarity and does not know what it means to love—it may know pleasure but it certainly does not know what it means to love. Fear destroys and makes the mind ugly.

There is physical fear and psychological fear. There is the physical fear of danger—like meeting a snake or coming upon a precipice. That fear, the physical fear of meeting danger, is it not intelligence? There is a precipice there—I see it and I immediately react, I do not go near it. Now is not that fear intelligence which says to me, "Be careful, there is danger"? That intelligence has been accumulated through time, others have fallen over or my mother or my friend has said, "Be careful of that precipice." So in that physical expression of fear there is memory and intelligence operating at the same time. Then there is the psychological fear of the physical fear that one has had, of having had a disease which has given a great deal of pain; having known pain, purely a physical phenomenon, we do not want it to be repeated again and we have the psychological fear of it although it is no longer actual. Now can that psychological fear be understood so as not to bring it into being at all? I have had pain—most of us do—it happened last week or a year ago. The pain was excruciating, I do not want it repeated and I am afraid it might come back. What has taken place there? Please follow this carefully. There is the memory of that pain and thought says, "Don't let it occur again, be careful." Thinking about the past pain brings fear of its repetition, thought brings fear upon itself. That is a particular form of fear, the fear of disease being repeated with its pain.

There are all the various psychological fears which derive from thought—fear of what the neighbor might say, fear of not being highly bourgeois and respectable, fear of not following the social morality—which is immorality—fear of losing a job, fear of loneliness, fear of anxiety—anxiety in itself is fear and so on—all the products of a life which is based on thought.

There are not only the conscious fears, but also the deep, hidden fears in the psyche, in the deeper layers of the mind. One may deal with the conscious fears, but the deep, hidden fears are more difficult. How is one to bring these unconscious, deep, hidden fears to the surface and expose them? Can the conscious mind do that? Can the conscious mind with its active thought uncover the unconscious, the hidden? (We are using the word "unconscious" nontechnically: not being conscious of, or knowing, the hidden layers—that is all.) Can the conscious mind—the mind that is trained to adjust itself to survive, to go on with things as they are—you know the conscious mind, how tricky it is—can that conscious mind uncover the whole content of the unconscious? I do not think it can. It may uncover a layer which it will translate according to its conditioning. But that very translation according to its conditioning will further prejudice the conscious mind, so that it is even less capable of examining the next layer completely.

One sees that the mere conscious effort to examine the deeper content of the mind becomes extremely difficult unless the surface mind is completely free from all conditioning, from all prejudice, from all fear—otherwise it is incapable of looking. One sees that that may be extremely difficult, probably completely impossible. So one asks: is there another way, altogether different?

Can the mind empty itself of all fear through analysis, self-analysis or professional analysis? In that is involved something else. When I analyze myself, look at myself, layer after layer, I examine, judge, evaluate; I say, "This is right," "This is wrong," "This I will keep," "This I won't keep." When I analyze, am I different from the thing I analyze? I have to answer it for myself, see what the truth of it is. The analyzer, is he different from the thing he is analyzing—say jealousy? He is not different, he is that jealousy, and he tries to divide himself off from the jealousy as the entity who says, "I am going to look at jealousy, get rid of it, or contact it." But jealousy and the analyzer are part of each other.

In the process of analysis time is involved, that is, I take many days or many years to analyze myself. At the end of many years I am still afraid. So, analysis is not the way. Analysis implies a great deal of time and when the house is burning you do not sit down and analyze, or go to the professional and say, "Please tell me all about myself"—you have to act. Analysis is a form of escape, laziness and inefficiency. (It may be all right for the neurotic to go to an analyst, but even then he is not completely at the end of his neuroses. But that is a different question.)

Analysis by the conscious of the unconscious is not the way. The mind has seen this and said to itself, "I will not analyze any more, I see the valuelessness of it"; "I will not resist fear any more." You follow what has happened to the mind? When it has discarded the traditional approach, the approach of analysis, resistance, time, then what has happened to the mind itself? The mind has become extraordinarily sharp. The mind has become, through the necessity of observation, extraordinarily intense, sharp, alive. It is asking: is there another approach to this problem of uncovering its whole content, the past, the racial inheritance, the family, the weight of the cultural and religious tradition, the product of two thousand or ten thousand years? Can the mind be free of all that, can the mind put away all that and therefore put away all fear?

So I have this problem, the problem which a sharpened mind—the mind having put aside every form of analysis which of necessity takes time and for which therefore there is no tomorrow—must resolve completely, now. Therefore there is no ideal; there is no question of a future, saying, "I will be free of it." Therefore the mind is now in a state of *complete attention*. It is no longer escaping, no longer inventing time as a way of resolving the problem, no longer using analysis, or resistance. Therefore the mind itself has a quality entirely new.

The psychologists say that you must dream, otherwise you will go mad. I ask myself, "Why should I dream at all?" Is there a way of living so that one does not dream at all?—for then, if one does not dream at all, the mind really has rest. It has been active all day, watching, listening, questioning, looking at the beauty of a cloud, the face of a beautiful person, the water, the movement of life, everything—it has been watching, watching; and when it goes to sleep it must have complete rest, otherwise on waking the next morning it is tired, it is still old.

So one asks is there a way of not dreaming at all so that the mind during sleep has complete rest and can come upon certain qualities which it cannot during the waking hours? It is possible only—and this is a fact, not a supposition, not a theory, not an invention, or a hope— it is possible only when you are completely awake during the day, watching every activity of your thought, your feeling, awake to every motive, to every intimation, every hint of that which is deep down, when you chatter, when you walk, when you listen to somebody, when you are watching your ambition, your jealousy, watching your response to the "glory of France," when you read a book which says "your religious beliefs are nonsense"—watching to see what is implied in belief. During the waking hours be completely awake, when you are sitting in the bus, when you are talking to your wife, to your children, to your friend, when you are smoking—why you are smoking —when you read a detective story—why you are reading it—when you go to a cinema—why—for excitement, for sex? When you see a beautiful tree or the movement of a cloud across the sky, be completely aware of what is happening within and without, then you will see, when you go to sleep, that you do not dream and when you wake the next morning the mind is fresh, intense, and alive.

Paris, April 13, 1969

8. The Transcendental

To penetrate into reality?
Tradition of meditation.
Reality and the still mind.

We have been talking about the chaos in the world, the great violence, the confusion, not only outwardly but inwardly. Violence is the result of fear and we went into the question of fear. I think we ought now to go into something that may be a little foreign to most of you: but it must be considered and not merely rejected, saying that it is an illusion, a fancy and so on.

Throughout history, man—realizing his life is very short, full of accidents, sorrow and inevitable death—has always formulated an idea which is called God. He realized, as we do now also, that life is transient and he wanted to experience something vastly great, supreme, to experience something not put together by the mind or by emotion; he wanted to experience, or feel his way into, a world that is entirely different, a world that transcends this, that lies beyond all misery and torture. And he hoped to find this transcendental world by seeking, searching it out. We ought to go into this question as to whether there is, or there is not, a reality—it doesn't matter what name one gives it—that is of an altogether different dimension. To penetrate into its depth one must naturally realize that it is not enough to merely understand at the verbal level— for the description is never the described, the word is never the thing. Can we penetrate into the mystery—if it is a mystery that man has always been trying to enter or capture, inviting it, holding it, worshiping it, becoming its devotee?

Life being what it is—rather shallow, empty, a tortuous affair without much meaning—one tries to invent a significance, give it a meaning. If one has a certain cleverness, the significance and the purpose of the invention become rather complex. And not finding the beauty, the love, or the sense of immensity, one may become cynical, not believing in anything. One sees it is rather absurd and illusory and without much meaning to merely invent an ideology, a formula, affirming that there is God or that there is not, when life has no meaning whatsoever—which is true the way we live, it has no meaning. So do not let us invent a meaning.

If we could go together and discover for ourselves if there is, or if there is not, a reality, which is not merely an intellectual or emotional invention, an escape. Man throughout history has said that there is a reality for which you must prepare, for which you must do certain things, discipline yourself, resist every form of temptation, control yourself, control sex, conform to a pattern established by religious authority, the saints and so on; or you must deny the world, withdraw into a monastery, to some cave where you can meditate, to be alone and not be tempted. One sees the absurdity of such striving; one sees that one cannot possibly escape from the world, from "what is," from the suffering, from the distraction, and from all that man has put together in science. And the theologies: one must obviously discard all theologies and all beliefs. If one does completely put aside every form of belief, then there is no fear whatsoever.

Knowing that social morality is no morality, that it is immoral, one sees that one must be extraordinarily moral, for after all, morality is only the bringing of order both within oneself and also without oneself; but that morality must be in action, not merely an ideational or conceptual morality, but actual moral behavior.

Is it possible to discipline oneself without suppression,

control, escape? The root meaning of the word "discipline" is "to learn," not to conform or become a disciple of somebody, not to imitate or suppress, but to learn. The very act of learning demands discipline—a discipline which is not imposed nor accommodating itself to some ideology—not the harsh austerity of the monk. Yet without a deep austerity our behavior in daily life only leads to disorder. One can see how essential it is to have complete order in oneself, like mathematical order, not relative, not comparative, not brought about by environmental influence. Behavior, which is righteousness, must be established so that the mind is in complete order. A mind that is tortured, frustrated, shaped by environment, conforming to the social morality, must in itself be confused; and a confused mind cannot discover what is true.

If the mind is to come upon that strange mystery—if there is such a thing—it must lay the foundation of a behavior, a morality, which is not that of society, a morality in which there is no fear whatsoever and which is therefore free. It is only then—after laying this deep foundation—that the mind can proceed to find out what meditation is, that quality of silence, of observation, in which the "observer" is not. If this basis of righteous behavior does not take place in one's life, in one's action, then meditation has very little meaning.

In the Orient there are many schools, systems and methods of meditation—including Zen and Yoga—which have been brought over to the West. One must be very clear in understanding this suggestion that through a method, through a system, through conforming to a certain pattern or tradition, the mind can come upon that reality. One can see how absurd the thing is, whether it is brought from the East or whether it is invented here. Method implies conformity, repetition; method implies someone who has reached a certain enlightenment, who says, do this and do not do that. And we, who are so eager to have that reality, follow, conform, obey, practice what we have been told, day after day, like a lot of machines. A dull insensitive mind, a mind that is not highly intelligent, can practice a method endlessly; it will become more and more dull, more and more stupid. It will have its own "experience" within the field of its own conditioning.

Some of you perhaps have been to the East and have studied meditation there. A whole tradition exists behind it. In India, throughout the whole of Asia, it exploded in the ancient days. That tradition even now still holds the mind, endless volumes are written on it. But any form of tradition—a carry-over from the past—which is used to find out if there is great reality, is obviously a waste of endeavor. The mind must be free of every form of spiritual tradition and sanction; otherwise one becomes utterly lacking in the highest form of intelligence.

Then what is meditation, if it is not traditional?—and it cannot be traditional, no one can teach you, you cannot follow a particular path, and say, "Along that path I will learn what meditation is." The whole meaning of meditation is in the mind becoming completely quiet; quiet, not only at the conscious level but also at the deep, secret, hidden levels of consciousness; so completely and utterly quiet so that thought is silent and does not wander all over the place. One of the teachings of the tradition of meditation, the traditional approach we are talking about, is that thought must be controlled; but that must be totally set aside and to set it aside one must look at it very closely, objectively, nonemotionally.

Tradition says you must have a guru, a teacher, to help you to meditate, he will tell you what to do. The West has its own form of tradition, of prayer, contemplation and confession. But in the whole principle that someone else knows and you do not know, that the one who knows is going to teach you, give you enlightenment, in that is implied authority, the master, the guru, the savior, the Son of God and so on. They know and you do not know; they say, follow this method, this system, do it day after day, practice and you will eventually get there—if you are lucky. Which means you are fighting with yourself all day long, trying to conform to a pattern, to a system, trying to suppress your own desires, your own appetites, your own envy, jealousies, ambitions. And so there is the conflict between what you are and what should be according to the system; this means there is effort; and a mind that is making an effort can never be quiet; through effort mind can never become completely still.

Tradition also says concentrate in order to control your thought. To concentrate is merely to resist, to build a wall around yourself, to protect an exclusive focusing on one idea, on a principle, a picture, or what you will. Tradition says you must go through that in order to find whatever you want to find. Tradition also says you must have no sex, you must not look at this world, as all the saints, who are more or less neurotic, have always said. And when you see—not merely verbally and intellectually, but actually—what is involved in all this—and you can see it only if you are not committed to it and can look at it objectively—then you discard it completely. One must discard it completely, for then the mind, in the very discarding, becomes free and therefore intelligent, aware, and not liable to be caught in illusions.

To meditate in the deepest sense of the word one must be virtuous, moral; not the morality of a pattern, of a practice, or of the social order, but the morality that comes naturally, inevitably, sweetly when you begin to understand yourself, when you are aware of your thoughts, your feelings, your activities, your appetites, your ambitions and so on—aware without any choice, merely observing. Out of that observation comes right action, which has nothing to do with conformity, or action according to an ideal. Then when that exists deeply in oneself, with its beauty and austerity in which there is not a particle of harshness—for harshness exists only when there is effort—when one has observed all the systems, all the methods, all the promises and looked at them objectively without like or dislike, then you can discard them altogether so that your mind is free from the past; then you can proceed to find out what meditation is.

If you have not actually laid the foundation, you can play with meditation but that has no meaning—it is like those people who go out to the East, go to some master who will tell them how to sit, how to breathe, what to do, this or that, and who come back and write a book, which is all sheer nonsense. One has to be a teacher to oneself and a disciple of oneself, there is no authority, there is only understanding.

Understanding is possible only when there is observation without the center as the observer. Have you ever observed, watched, tried to find out, what understanding is? Understanding is not an intellectual process; understanding is not an intuition or a feeling. When one says, "I understand something very clearly," there is an observation out of complete silence—it is only then there is understanding. When you say, "I understand something," you mean that the mind listens very quietly, neither agreeing nor disagreeing; that state listens completely—it is only then there is understanding and that understanding is action. It is not that there is understanding first and then action follows afterward, it is simultaneous, one movement.

So meditation—that word which is so heavily loaded by tradition—is to bring, without effort, without any form of compulsion, the mind and the brain to their highest capacity, which is intelligence, which is to be highly sensitive. The brain is quiet; that repository of the past, evolved through a million years, which is continuously and incessantly active—that brain is quiet.

Is it at all possible for the brain, which is reacting all the time, responding to the least stimulus, according to its conditioning, to be still? The traditionalists say, it can be made still by proper breathing, by practicing awareness. This again involves the question, "who" is the entity that controls, that practices, that shapes the brain? Is it not thought, which says, "I am the observer and I am going to control the brain, put an end to thought"? Thought breeds the thinker.

Is it possible for the brain to be completely quiet? It is part of meditation to find out, not to be told how to do it; nobody can tell us how to do it. Your brain—which is so heavily conditioned through culture, through every form of experience, the brain which is the result of vast evolution—can it be so still?—because without that, whatever it sees or experiences will be distorted, will be translated according to its conditioning.

What part does sleep play in meditation, in living? It is quite an interesting question; if you have gone into it yourself you will have discovered a great deal. As we said the other day: dreams are unnecessary. We said: the mind, the brain, must be completely aware during the day—attentive to what is happening both outwardly and inwardly, aware of the inward reactions to the outer with its strains evoking reactions, attentive to the intimation of the unconscious—and then at the end of the day it must take all that into account. If you do not take all that has happened into account at the end of the day, the brain has to work at night, when you are asleep, to bring order into itself—which is obvious. If you have done all this, then when you sleep you are learning quite a different thing altogether, you are learning at a different dimension altogether; and that is part of meditation.

There is the laying of the foundation of behavior, in which action is love. There is the discarding of all traditions, so that the mind is completely free; and the brain is completely quiet. If you have gone into it you will see that the brain can be quiet, not through any trick, not through taking a drug, but through that active and also passive awareness throughout the day. And if you have taken stock at the end of the day, of what has happened, and therefore brought order, then when there is sleep, the brain is quiet, learning with a different movement.

So this whole body, the brain, everything, is quiet, without any form of distortion; it is only then if there is any reality that such a mind can receive it. It cannot be invited, that immensity—if there is such an immensity, if there is the nameless, the transcendental, if there is such a thing—it is only such a mind that can see the false or the truth of that reality.

You might say, "What has all this to do with living? I have to live this everyday life, go to the office, wash dishes, travel in a crowded bus with all the noise—what has meditation to do with all this?" Yet after all, meditation is the understanding of life, the life every day with all its complexity, misery, sorrow, loneliness, despair, the drive to become famous, successful, the fear, envy—to understand all that is meditation. Without understanding it, the mere attempt to find the mystery is utterly empty, it has no value. It is like a disordered life, a disordered mind, trying to find mathematical order. Meditation has everything to do with life; it isn't going off into some emotional, ecstatic state. There is ecstasy which is not pleasure; that ecstasy comes only when there is this mathematical order in oneself, which is absolute. Meditation is the way of life, every day—only then, that which is imperishable, which has no time, can come into being.

Questioner: Who is the observer that is aware of his own reactions? What is the energy that is used?

Krishnamurti: Have you looked at anything without reaction? Have you looked at a tree, at the face of a woman, at the mountain, or the cloud, or the light on the water, just to observe it, without translating it into like or dislike, pleasure or pain—just to observe it? In such observation, when you are completely attentive, is there an observer? Do it, Sir, do not ask me—if you do it you will find out. Observe reactions, without judging, evaluating, distorting, be so completely attentive to every reaction and in that attention you will see that there is no observer or thinker or experiencer at all.

Then the second question: to change anything in one-self, to bring about a transformation, a revolution in the psyche, what energy is used? How is that energy to be had? We have energy now, but in tension, in contradiction, in conflict; there is energy in the battle between two desires, between what I must do and what I should do—that consumes a great deal of energy. But if there is no contradiction whatsoever then you have abundance of energy. Look at one's own life, actually do look at it: it is a contradiction; you want to be peaceful and you hate somebody; you want to love and you are ambitious. This contradiction breeds conflict, struggle; that struggle wastes energy. If there is no contradiction whatsoever you have the supreme energy to transform yourself. One asks: how is it possible to have no contradiction between the "observer" and the "observed," between the "experiencer" and the "experience," between love and hate?—these dualities, how is it possible to live without them? It is possible when there is only the fact and nothing else—the fact that you hate, that you are violent, and not its opposite as idea. When you are afraid you develop the opposite, courage, which is resistance, contradiction, effort, and strain. But when you understand completely what fear is and do not escape into the opposite, when you give your whole attention to fear, then there is not only its cessation, psychologically, but also you have the energy that is needed to confront it. The traditionalists say, "You must have this energy, therefore do not be sexual, do not be worldly, concentrate, put your mind on God, leave the world, do not be tempted"—all in order to have this energy. But one is still a human being with appetites, burning inside with sexual, biological urges, wanting to do this, controlling, forcing and all the rest of it—therefore wasting energy. But if you live with the fact and nothing else—if you are angry, understand it and not "how to be not angry," go into it, be with it, live with it, give complete attention to it—you will see that you have this energy in abundance. It is this energy that keeps the mind clear, your heart open, so that there is abundance of love—not ideas, not sentiment.

Questioner: What do you mean by ecstasy, can you describe it? You said ecstasy is not pleasure, love is not pleasure?

Krishnamurti: What is ecstasy? When you look at a cloud, at the light in that cloud, there is beauty. Beauty is passion. To see the beauty of a cloud or the beauty of light on a tree, there must be passion, there must be intensity. In this intensity, this passion, there is no sentiment whatsoever, no feeling of like or dislike. Ecstasy is not personal; ecstasy is not yours or mine, just as love is not yours or mine. When there is pleasure it is yours or mine. When there is that meditative mind it has its own ecstasy—which is not to be described, not to be put into words.

Questioner: Are you saying that there is no good and bad, that all reactions are good—are you saying that?

Krishnamurti: No, Sir, I did not say that. I said, observe your reaction, do not call it good or bad. When you call it good or bad you bring about contradiction. Have you ever looked at your wife—I am sorry to keep at it—without the image that you have about her, the image that you have put together over thirty or so years? You have an image about her and she has an image about you; these images have relationship; you and she do not have relationship. These images come into being when you are not attentive in your relationship—it is inattention that breeds images. Can you look at your wife without condemning, evaluating, saying she is right, she is wrong, just observe without bringing in your prejudices? Then you will see there is a totally different kind of action that comes from that observation.

Paris, April 24, 1969

PART IV

9. On Violence

**What is violence? Imposition at the root of
psychological violence. Need to observe.
Inattention.**

Krishnamurti: The intention of these discussions is to be
creatively observant—to watch ourselves creatively as we
are speaking. All of us should contribute to any subject
that we want to discuss and there must be a certain
frankness—not rudeness or a rough exposing of another's
stupidity or intelligence; but each one of us should par-
take in discussing a certain issue with all its content. In
the very statement of anything that we feel, or inquire
into, there must be a sense of perceiving something new.
That is creation, not the repetition of the old, but the
expression of the new in the discovery of ourselves as we
are expressing ourselves in words. Then I think these discussions will be worthwhile.

Questioner (1): Can we go more deeply into this question
of energy and how it is wasted?

Questioner (2): You have been talking about violence, the
violence of war, the violence in how we treat people, the
violence of how we think and look at other people. But
how about the violence of self-preservation? If I were attacked by a wolf, I would defend myself passionately with
all the forces I have. Is it possible to be violent in *one* part
of us and not in another?

Krishnamurti: A suggestion has been made with regard to violence, distorting ourselves to conform to a particular pattern of society, or morality; but there is also the question of self-preservation. Where is the demarcation between self-preservation—which sometimes may demand violence—and other forms of violence? Do you want to discuss that?

Audience: Yes.

Krishnamurti: First of all may I suggest that we discuss the various forms of psychological violence, and then see what is the place of self-preservation when attacked. I wonder what you think of violence? What is violence to you?

Questioner (1): It's a type of defense.

Questioner (2): It's a disturbance of my comfort.

Krishnamurti: What does violence, the feeling, the word, the nature of violence mean to you?

Questioner (1): It is aggression.

Questioner (2): If you are frustrated you get violent.

Questioner (3): If man is incapable of accomplishing something, then he gets violent.

Questioner (4): Hate, in the sense of overcoming.

Krishnamurti: What does violence mean to you?

Questioner (1): An expression of danger, when the "me" comes in.

Questioner (2): Fear.

102

Questioner (3): Surely in violence you are hurting some-body or something, either mentally or physically.

Krishnamurti: Do you know violence because you know nonviolence? Would you know what violence was without its opposite? Because you know states of nonviolence, do you therefore recognize violence? How do you know violence? Because one is aggressive, competitive, and one sees the effects of all that, which is violence, one construes a state of nonviolence. If there were no opposite, would you know what violence was?

Questioner: I wouldn't label it but I'd feel something.

Krishnamurti: Does that feeling exist or come into being because you know violence?

Questioner: I think that violence causes us pain; it is an unhealthy feeling we want to get rid of. That's why we want to become nonviolent.

Krishnamurti: I don't know anything about violence, nor about nonviolence. I don't start with any concept or formula. I really don't know what violence means. I want to find out.

Questioner: The experience of having been hurt and attacked makes one want to protect oneself.

Krishnamurti: Yes, I understand that; that has been suggested before. I am still trying to find out what violence is. I want to investigate, I want to explore it, I want to uproot it, change it—you follow?

Questioner: Violence is lack of love.

Krishnamurti: Do you know what love is?

Questioner: I think that all these things come from us.

Krishnamurti: Yes, that's just it.

Questioner: Violence comes from us.

Krishnamurti: That's right. I want to find out whether it comes from outside or from inside.

Questioner: It's a form of protection.

Krishnamurti: Let us go slowly, please; it is quite a serious problem and the whole world is involved in it.

Questioner: Violence wastes part of my energy.

Krishnamurti: Everybody has talked about violence and nonviolence. People say, "You must live violently," or seeing the effect of it, they say, "You must live peacefully." We have heard so many things, from books, from preachers, from educators and others; but I want to discover whether it is possible to find out the nature of violence and what place—if any—it has in life. What is it that makes one violent, aggressive, competitive? And is violence involved in conformity to a pattern, however noble? Is violence part of the discipline imposed by oneself or by society? Is violence conflict within and without? I want to find out what is the origin, the beginning, of violence; otherwise I am just spinning a lot of words. Is it natural to be violent in the psychological sense? (We will consider the physiopsychological states afterward.) Inwardly, is violence aggression, anger, hate, conflict, suppression, conformity? And is conformity based on this constant struggle to find, to achieve, to become, to arrive, to self-realize, to be noble, and all the rest of it? All that lies in the psychological field. If we cannot go into it very deeply then we shan't be able to understand how we can bring about a different state in our daily life, which demands a certain amount of self-preservation. Right? So let us start from there.

What would you consider is violence—not verbally, but actually, inwardly?

Questioner (1): It's violating something else. It imposes upon something.

Questioner (2): What about rejection?

Krishnamurti: Let's take imposing first, violating "what is." I am jealous and I impose on that an idea of not being jealous: "I must *not* be jealous." The imposition, the violating of "what is," is violence. We'll start little by little, perhaps in that one sentence the whole thing may be covered. The "what is" is always moving, it is not static. I violate that by imposing on it something which I think "should be."

Questioner: Do you mean that when I feel anger I think anger should not be and, instead of being angry, I hold it back? Is that violence? Or is it violence when I express it?

Krishnamurti: Look at something in this: I am angry and to give release to it I hit you and that brings about a chain of reactions, so that you hit me back. The very expression of that anger is violence. And if I impose upon the fact that I am angry something else, that is "not to be angry," is that not also violence?

Questioner: I would agree with that very general definition but the imposition must happen in a brutal way. This is what makes it violent. If you impose it in a gradual way, then it would not be violent.

Krishnamurti: I understand, Sir. If you apply the imposition with gentleness, with tact, then it is not violence. I violate the fact that I hate by gradually, gently, suppressing it. That, the gentleman says, would not be violent. But whether you do it violently or gently, the fact is you impose something else on "what is." Do we more or less agree to that?

Questioner: No.

Krishnamurti: Let's examine it. Say I am ambitious to become the greatest poet in the world (or whatever it is), and I am frustrated because I can't. This frustration, this very ambition, is a form of violence against the fact that I am not. I feel frustrated because you are better than I am. Doesn't that breed violence?

Questioner: All action against a person or against a thing is violence.

Krishnamurti: Do please look at the difficulty involved in this. There is the fact, and the violation of that fact by another action. Say, for instance, I don't like the Russians, or the Germans, or the Americans and I impose my particular opinion, or political evaluation; that is a form of violence. When I impose on you, that is violence. When I compare myself with you (who are much greater, more intelligent), I am violating myself—isn't that so? I am violent. At school "B" is compared with "A," who is much better at his exams and passes brilliantly. The teacher says to "B," "You must be like him." Therefore when he compares "B" with "A" there is violence and he destroys "B." See what is implied in this fact, that when I impose on "what is" the "what should be" (the ideal, the perfection, the image and so on), there is violence.

Questioner (1): I feel in myself that if there is any resistance, anything that might destroy, then violence comes into being, but also, that if you don't resist, you could be violating yourself.

Questioner (2): Isn't all this dealing with the self, the "me" which is the root of all violence?

Questioner (3): Suppose I take your word for all this. Suppose you hate somebody and would like to eliminate that hate. There are two approaches: the violent approach and the nonviolent approach. If you impose upon your own being to eliminate that hate you will do violence to yourself. If on the other hand you take the time, take the trouble to get to know your feelings and the object of your hate, you will gradually overcome that hate. Then you will have solved the problem in a nonviolent way.

Krishnamurti: I think that's fairly clear, Sir, isn't it? We are not trying at present to find out how to dispose of violence, in a violent way or a nonviolent way, but what brings about this violence in us. What is violence in us, psychologically?

Questioner: In the imposition, isn't there a breaking up of something? Then one feels uncomfortable and one begins to get more violent.

Krishnamurti: The breaking up of one's ideas, one's way of life and so on, that makes for discomfort. That discomfort brings about violence.

Questioner (1): Violence can come from outside or from inside. I generally blame this violence on the outside.

Questioner (2): Is not the root of violence the result of fragmentation?

Krishnamurti: Please, there are so many ways of showing what violence is, or what the causes are. Can't we see one simple fact and begin from there, slowly? Can't we see that any form of imposition, of the parent over the child, or the child over the parent, of the teacher over the pupil, of the society, or of the priest, all these are forms of violence? Can't we agree on that and begin there?

Questioner: That comes from the outside.

Krishnamurti: We do that not only outwardly but also inwardly. I say to myself "I am angry," and I impose on that an idea that I must not be angry. We say that is violence. Outwardly, when a dictator suppresses the people, that is violence. When I suppress what I feel because I am afraid, because it is not noble, because it is not pure, and so on, that is also violence. So the nonacceptance of the fact of "what is" brings about this imposition. If I accept the fact that I am jealous and offer no resistance to it, there is no imposition; then I will know what to do with it. There is no violence in it.

Questioner: You are saying education is violence.

Krishnamurti: I do. Is there not a way of educating without violence?

Questioner: According to tradition, no.

Krishnamurti: The problem is: by nature, in my thoughts, in the way I live, I am a violent human being, aggressive, competitive, brutal and all the rest of it—I am that. And I say to myself, "How am I to live differently?" because violence breeds tremendous antagonism and destruction in the world. I want to understand it and be free of it, live differently. So I ask myself, "What is this violence in me? Is it frustration, because I want to be famous and I know I can't be, therefore I hate people who are famous?" I am jealous and I want to be nonjealous and I hate this state of jealousy with all its anxiety and fear and annoyance, therefore I suppress it. I do all this and I realize it is a way of violence. Now I want to find out if that is inevitable; or if there is a way of understanding it, looking at it, coming to grips with it so that I shall live differently. So I must find out what violence is.

Questioner: It's a reaction.

Krishnamurti: You are too quick. Does that help me to understand the nature of my violence? I want to go into it, I want to find out. I see that as long as there is a duality—that is, violence and nonviolence—there must be conflict and therefore more violence. As long as I impose on the fact that I am stupid the idea that I must be clever, there is the beginning of violence. When I compare myself with you, who are much more than I am, that's also violence. Comparison, suppression, control—all those indicate a form of violence. I am made like that. I compare, I suppress, I am ambitious. Realizing that, how am I to live nonviolently? I want to find a way of living without all this strife.

Questioner: Isn't it the "me" and the self that is against the fact?

Krishnamurti: We'll come to that. See the fact, see what is happening first. My whole life, from when I was educated till now, has been a form of violence. The society in which I live is a form of violence. Society tells me to conform, accept, do this, not do that, and I follow it. That is a form of violence. And when I revolt against society, that also is a form of violence (revolt in the sense that I don't accept the values which society has laid down). I revolt against it and then create my own values, which become the pattern; and that pattern is imposed on others or on myself, which becomes another form of violence. I live that kind of life. That is: I am violent. Now what shall I do?

Questioner: First, you should ask yourself why you don't want to be violent anymore.

Krishnamurti: Because I see what violence has done in the world as it is; wars outwardly, conflict within, conflict in relationship. Objectively and inwardly I see this battle going on and I say, "Surely there must be a different way of living."

Questioner: Why do you dislike that state of affairs?

Krishnamurti: It is very destructive.

Questioner: Then this means that you yourself have already given the highest value to love.

Krishnamurti: I have given no value to anything. I am just observing.

Questioner: If you dislike, then you have given values.

Krishnamurti: I am not giving values, I observe. I observe war is destructive.

Questioner: What's wrong with that?

Krishnamurti: I don't say it is right or wrong.

Questioner: Then why do you want to change it?

Krishnamurti: I want to change it because my son gets killed in a war, and I ask, "Isn't there a way of living without killing one another?"

Questioner: So all you want to do is to experiment with a different way of living, then compare the new way of living with what is going on now.

Krishnamurti: No, Sir. I don't compare. I have expressed all this. I see my son gets killed in a war and I say, "Is there not a different way of living?" I want to find out if there is a way in which violence doesn't exist.

Questioner: But supposing—

Krishnamurti: No supposition, Sir. My son gets killed and I want to find a way of living in which other sons aren't killed.

Questioner: So what you want is one or the other of two possibilities.

Krishnamurti: There are a dozen possibilities.

Questioner: Your urge to find another way of living is so great that you want to adopt another way—whatever it is. You want to experiment with it and compare it.

Krishnamurti: No, Sir, I am afraid you are insisting on something which I have not made clear.

Either we accept the way of life as it is, with violence and all the rest of it; or we say there must be a different way which human intelligence can find, where violence doesn't exist. That's all. And we say this violence will exist so long as comparison, suppression, conformity, the disciplining of oneself according to a pattern is the way of life. In this there is conflict and therefore violence.

Questioner: Why does confusion arise? Isn't it created around the "I"?

Krishnamurti: We'll come to that, Sir.

Questioner: The thing underneath violence, the root, the essence of violence, is in fact affecting. Owing to the fact that we exist, we affect the rest of existence. I am here. By breathing the air I affect the existence within it. So I claim that the essence of violence is the fact of affecting, which is inherent in existence. When we affect in discord, in disharmony, we call that violence. But if we harmonize with it, then that's the other side of violence—but it is still affecting. One is "affecting against," which is violating, the other is affecting with.

Krishnamurti: Sir, may I ask something? Are you concerned with violence? Are you involved in violence? Are you concerned about this violence in yourself and in the world in the sense that you feel, "I can't live this way"?

Questioner: When we revolt against violence we form a problem because revolt is violence.

Krishnamurti: I understand, Sir, but how do we proceed with this subject?

Questioner: I don't agree with society. Revolt against ideas —money, efficiency and so on—is my form of violence.

Krishnamurti: Yes, I understand. Therefore that rebellion against the present culture, education and so on, is violence.

Questioner: That's how I see my violence.

Krishnamurti: Yes, therefore what will you do with that? That's what we are trying to discuss.

Questioner: That is what I want to know.

Krishnamurti: I want to know about this too. So let us stick to it.

Questioner: If I have a problem with a person, I can understand it much more clearly. If I hate someone I know it; I react against it. But this is not possible with society.

Krishnamurti: Let us take this, please. I rebel against the present moral structure of society. I realize that mere rebellion against this morality, without finding out what is true morality, is violence. What is true morality? Unless I find that out and live it, merely to rebel against the structure of a social morality has very little meaning.

Questioner: Sir, you can't know violence unless you live it.

Krishnamurti: Oh! Are you saying I must live violently before I can understand the other?

Questioner: You said to understand true morality you must live it. You must live violently to see what love is.

Krishnamurti: When you say I must live that way, you are already imposing on me an idea of what you think love is.

Questioner: That's repeating your words.

Krishnamurti: Sir, there is the social morality against which I rebel because I see how absurd it is. What is true morality in which there is no violence?

Questioner: Isn't true morality controlling violence? Surely there is violence in everybody, people—so-called higher beings—are controlling it, in nature it is always there; whether it is a thunderstorm or a wild animal killing another, or a tree dying, violence is everywhere.

Krishnamurti: There may be a higher form of violence, more subtle, more tenuous, and there are the brutal forms of violence. The whole of life is violence, the little and the big. If one wants to find out whether it is possible to step out of this whole structure of violence, one has to go into it. That's what we are trying to do.

Questioner: Sir, what do you mean by "going into it"?

113

Krishnamurti: I mean by "going into it," first the examination, the exploration of "what is." To explore, there must be freedom from any conclusion, from any prejudice. Then with that freedom I look at the problem of violence. That is "going into."

Questioner: Then does something happen?

Krishnamurti: No, nothing happens.

Questioner: I find that my reaction against war is "I don't want to fight," but I find the thing I do is to try to keep away, live in another country, or keep away from the people I don't like. I just keep away from American society.

Krishnamurti: She says, "I am not a demonstrator or protestor but I don't live in the country in which there is all this. I keep away from people whom I don't like." All this is a form of violence. Please do let us pay a little attention to this. Let us give our minds to understand this question. What is a man to do, who sees the whole pattern of behavior, political, religious, and economic, in which violence is involved to a greater or smaller degree, when he feels caught in the trap which he himself has created?

Questioner: May I suggest that there is no violence, but thinking makes it so.

Krishnamurti: Oh! I kill somebody and I think about it and therefore it is violent. No, Sir, aren't we playing with words? Couldn't we go into this a little more? We have seen that whenever I impose upon myself, psychologically, an idea or a conclusion, that breeds violence. (We'll take that for the moment.) I am cruel—verbally and in feeling. I impose on that, saying "I must not," and I realize that is a form of violence. How am I to deal with this feeling of cruelty without imposing something else on it? Can I understand it without suppressing it, without running away from it, without any form of escape or substitution? Here is a fact—I am cruel. That is a problem to me and no amount of explanation, saying "You should, you should not," will solve it. Here is an issue which affects me and I want to resolve it, because I see there may be a different way of living. So I say to myself, "How can I be free of this cruelty without conflict," because the moment I introduce conflict in getting rid of cruelty, I have already brought violence into being. So first I must be very clear about what conflict implies. If there is any conflict with regard to cruelty—of which I want to be free—in that very conflict there is the breeding of violence. How am I to be free of cruelty without conflict?

Questioner: Accept it.

Krishnamurti: I wonder what we mean by accepting our cruelty. There it is! I am not accepting or denying it. What is the good of saying "Accept it"? It is a fact that I have a brown skin—it is so. Why should I accept it or reject it? The fact is I am cruel.

Questioner: If I see I am cruel I accept it, I understand it; but also I am afraid of acting cruelly and of going along with it.

Krishnamurti: Yes. I said, "I am cruel." I neither accept nor reject it. It is a fact; and it is another fact, that when there is conflict in getting rid of cruelty there is violence. So I have to deal with two things: violence, cruelty, and the ridding myself of it without effort. What am I to do? All my life struggle and fight.

Questioner: The question is not violence, but the creation of an image.

Krishnamurti: That image gets imposed upon, or one imposes that image on "what is"—right?

Questioner: It comes from ignorance of one's true being.

Krishnamurti: I don't quite know what you mean by "true being."

Questioner: I mean by that one is not separate from the world, one *is* the world and therefore one is responsible for the violence that goes on outside.

Krishnamurti: Yes. He says, true being is to recognize that one is the world and the world is oneself, and that cruelty and violence are not something different, but part of one. Is that what you mean, Sir?

Questioner: No. Part of the ignorance.

Krishnamurti: So you are saying there is the true self and there is ignorance? There are two states, the true being and it getting covered over by ignorance. Why? This is an old Indian theory. How do you know that there is a true being which is covered over by illusion and ignorance?

Questioner: If we realize that the problems we have are in terms of opposites, all problems will disappear.

Krishnamurti: All one has to do is not to think in opposites. Do we do that, or is it just an idea?

Questioner: Sir, isn't duality inherent in thought?

Krishnamurti: We come to a point and go away from it. I know I am cruel—for various psychological reasons. That is a fact. How shall I be free without effort?

Questioner: What do you mean by "without effort"?

Krishnamurti: I explained what I mean by effort. If I suppress it there is effort involved in the sense that there is contradiction: the cruelty and the desire not to be cruel. There is conflict between "what is" and "what should be."

Questioner: If I really look at it I can't be cruel.

Krishnamurti: I want to find out, not accept statements. I want to find out if it is at all possible to be free of cruelty. Is it possible to be free of it without suppression, without running away, trying to force it? What is one to do?

Questioner: The only thing to do is to expose it.

Krishnamurti: To expose it I must let it come out, let it show itself—not in the sense of becoming more cruel. Why don't I let it come out? First of all I am frightened of it. I don't know if by letting it come out I might not become more cruel. And if I expose it, am I capable of understanding it? Can I look at it very carefully, which means attentively? I can do it only if my energy, my interest and urgency coincide at this moment of exposure. At this moment I must have the urgency to understand it, I must have a mind without any kind of distortion. I must have tremendous energy to look. And these three must take place instantly at the moment of exposure. Which means, I am sensitive enough and free enough to have this vital energy, intensity and attention. How do I have that intense attention? How do I come by it?

Questioner: If we come to that point of wanting to understand it desperately, then we have this attention.

Krishnamurti: I understand. I am just saying, "Is it possible to be attentive?" Wait, see the implications of it, see what is involved in it. Don't give meanings, don't bring in a new set of words. Here I am. I don't know what attention means. Probably I have never given attention to anything, because most of my life I am inattentive. Suddenly you come along and say, "Look, be attentive about cru-

117

elty"; and I say, "I will"—but what does it mean? How am I to bring about this state of attention? Is there a method? If there is a method and I can practice to become attentive, it will take time. And during that time I continue to be inattentive and therefore bring more destruction. So all this must take place instantly!

I am cruel. I won't suppress, I won't escape; it doesn't mean that I am determined not to escape, it doesn't mean that I have made up my mind not to suppress it. But I see and understand intelligently that suppression, control, escape, do not solve the problem; therefore I have put those aside. Now I have this intelligence, which has come into being by understanding the futility of suppression, of escape, of trying to overcome. With this intelligence I am examining, I am looking at cruelty. I realize that to look at it, there must be a great deal of attention and to have that attention I must be very careful of my inattention. So my concern is to be aware of inattention. What does that mean? Because if I try to practice attention, it becomes mechanical, stupid, there is no meaning to it; but if I become attentive, or aware of lack of attention, then I begin to find out how attention comes into being. Why am I inattentive to other people's feelings, to the way I talk, the way I eat, to what people say and do? By understanding the negative state I shall come to the positive, which is attention. So I am examining, trying to understand how this inattention comes into being.

This is a very serious question because the whole world is burning. If I am part of that world and that world is me, I must put an end to the fire. So we are stranded with this problem. Because it is lack of attention that has brought about all this chaos in the world. One sees the curious fact that inattention is negation—lack of attention, lack of "being there" at the moment. How is it possible to be so completely aware of inattention that it becomes attention? How am I to become completely, instantly, aware of this cruelty in me, with great energy, so that there is no friction, no contradiction, so that it is complete, whole?

How do I bring this about? We said it is possible only when there is complete attention; and that complete attention does not exist because our life is spent wasting energy in inattention.

Saanen, Switzerland, August 3, 1969

10. On Radical Change

What is the instrument that looks?

Man has not changed very deeply. We are talking about the radical revolution in man, not the imposition of another pattern of behavior over the old one. We are concerned only with the basic change in what is actually going on inwardly in ourselves. As we said, the world and ourselves are not two different entities, the world is us and we are the world. To bring about a great change at the very root of our being, a revolution, a mutation, a transformation—it doesn't matter what word one uses—that is what we are involved in during these discussions.

We were asking yesterday: can one look at oneself clearly, without any distortion—distortion being the desire to evaluate, to judge, to achieve, to get rid of "what is"? All that prevents clear perception, prevents one from looking exactly and intimately at "what is." So I think this morning we should spend some time in discussing, or talking over together, the nature of observation, the way to look, to listen, to see. We shall try to find out whether it is at all possible to see, not only with one part of our being, visual, intellectual, or emotional. Is it at all possible to observe very closely without any distortion? It may be worthwhile to go into that. What is it to see? Can we look at ourselves, look at the basic fact of ourselves—which is greed, envy, anxiety, fear, hypocrisy, deception, ambition —can we just watch that, without any distortion?

Can we this morning spend some time trying to learn what it is to look? Learning is a constant movement, a constant renewal. It is not "having learned" and looking from there. By listening to what is being said and by watching ourselves a little bit, we learn something, we experience something; and from that learning and experiencing we look. We look with the memory of what we have learned and with what we have experienced; with that memory in mind we look. Therefore it is not looking, it is not learning. Learning implies a mind that learns each time anew. So it is always fresh to learn. Bearing that in mind we are not concerned with the cultivation of memory but rather to observe and see what actually takes place. We will try to be very alert, very attentive, so that what we have seen and what we have learned doesn't become a memory with which we look, and which is already a distortion. Look each time as though it were the first time! To look, to observe "what is" with a memory, means that memory dictates or shapes or directs your observation, and therefore it is already distorted. Can we go on from there?

We want to find out what it means to observe. The scientist may look at something through a microscope and observe closely; there is an outside object and he is looking at it without any prejudice, though with some knowledge which he must have to look. But here we are looking at the whole structure, at the whole movement of living, at the whole being which is "myself." It must be looked at not intellectually, not emotionally, nor with any conclusion about right or wrong, or that "this must not be"; "this should be." So before we can look intimately, we must be aware of this process of evaluation, judgment, forming conclusions, which is going on and which will prevent observation.

We are now concerned not with looking, but with what it is that is looking. Is the instrument that is looking spotted, distorted, tortured, burdened? What is important is not the seeing, but the observation of yourself who is the instrument that is looking. If I have a conclusion, for instance nationalism, and look with that deep conditioning, that tribal exclusiveness called nationalism, obviously I look with a great deal of prejudice; therefore I can't see clearly. Or if I am afraid to look, then that obviously is a distorted look. Or if I am ambitious for enlightenment, or for a bigger position, or whatever it is, then that also prevents the clarity of perception. One has to be aware of all that, aware of the instrument that is looking and whether it is clean.

Questioner: If one looks and finds that the instrument is not clean, what does one do then?

Krishnamurti: Please follow this carefully. We said observe "what is," the basic egoistic, self-centered activity, that which resists, which is frustrated, which becomes angry—observe all that. Then we said watch the instrument that is observing, find out whether that instrument is clean. We have moved from the fact to the instrument that is going to look. We are examining whether that instrument is clean, and we find that it is not clean. Then what are we to do? There is the sharpening of intelligence. I was concerned before to observe only the fact, the "what is"; I was watching it, and I moved away from that and said, "I must watch the instrument that is looking, whether it is clean." In that very questioning there is an intelligence—you are following all this? Therefore there is a sharpening of intelligence, a sharpening of the mind, of the brain.

Questioner: Doesn't this imply that there is a level of consciousness where there is no division, no conditioning?

Krishnamurti: I don't know what it implies. I am just moving little by little. The movement is not a fragmentary movement. It is not broken up. Before, when I looked I had no intelligence. I said, "I must change it"; "I must not change it"; "This must not be"; "This is good, this is bad"; "This should be"—all that. With those conclusions I looked and nothing happened. Now I realize the instrument must be extraordinarily clean to look. So it is one constant movement of intelligence, not a fragmentary state. I want to go on with this.

Questioner: Is this intelligence itself energy? If it is dependent on something it will fizzle out.

Krishnamurti: Don't bother for the moment; leave the question of energy alone.

Questioner: You have already got it, whereas to us it seems refinement upon refinement, but the drive is the same.

Krishnamurti: Yes. Is that what is taking place—refinement? Or has the mind, the brain, the whole being, become very dull through various means as pressures and activities and so on? And we are saying that the whole being must be awakened completely.

Questioner: This is the tricky bit.

Krishnamurti: Wait, I am coming to it, you will see it. Intelligence has no evolution. Intelligence is not the product of time. Intelligence is this quality of sensitive awareness of "what is." My mind is dull and I say, "I must look at myself," and this dull mind is trying to look at itself. Obviously it sees nothing. It either resists or rejects, or conforms; it is a very respectable mind, a bourgeois little mind that is looking.

Questioner: You began to speak of ideological systems of morality and now you go further and suggest that we should use self-observation, that all other systems are futile. Is this not also an ideology?

Krishnamurti: No, Sir. I say on the contrary, if you look with any ideology, including mine, then you are lost, then you are not looking at all. You have so many ideologies, respectable, not respectable, and all the rest of it; with those ideologies in your brain, in your heart, you are looking. Those ideologies have made the brain and the mind and your whole being dull. Now the dull mind looks. And obviously the dull mind, whatever it looks at, whether it meditates, or goes to the moon, it is still a dull mind. So that dull mind observes and somebody comes along and says, "Look, my friend, you are dull, what you see will be equally dull; because your mind is dull, what you see will inevitably be dull also." That is a great discovery, that a dull mind looking at something which is extraordinarily vital has made the thing it looks at also dull.

Questioner: But the same thing keeps reaching out.

Krishnamurti: Wait, go slowly, if you don't mind. Just move step by step with the speaker.

Questioner: If a dull mind recognizes that it is dull, it is not so dull.

Krishnamurti: I *don't* recognize it! That would be excellent if the dull mind recognized that is was dull, but it doesn't. Either it tries to polish itself more and more, by becoming learned, scientific, and all the rest of it, or if it is aware that it is dull it says, "This dull mind cannot look clearly." So the next question is: "How can this dull, spotted mind become extraordinarily intelligent, so that the instrument through which one looks is very clean?"

Questioner: Are you saying that when the mind puts the question in that way, it has put an end to the dullness? Can one do the right things for the wrong reasons?

Krishnamurti: No. I wish you would leave your conclusion and find out what the speaker is saying.

Questioner: No, sir. You stay with me.

Krishnamurti: What you are saying is this: you are trying to get hold of something, which will make the mind which is dull much sharper, clearer. I don't. I am saying: watch the dullness.

Questioner: Without the continual movement?

Krishnamurti: To watch the dull mind without the continual movement of distortion—how does that happen? My dull mind looks; therefore there is nothing to see. I ask myself, "How is it possible to make the mind bright?" Has this question come into being because I have compared the dull mind with another, clever mind, saying, "I must be like it"? You follow? That very comparison is the continuation of the dull mind.

Questioner: Can the dull mind compare itself with a clever one?

Krishnamurti: Doesn't it always compare itself with some bright mind? That's what we call evolution, don't we?

Questioner: The dull mind doesn't compare, it asks, "Why should I?" Or you can put it a little differently: one believes that if one can be a little cleverer one will get something more.

Krishnamurti: Yes, that's the same thing. So I have discovered something. The dull mind says, "I am dull through comparison, I am dull because that man is clever." It is not aware that it is dull in itself. There are two different states. If I am aware that I am dull because you are bright, that's one thing. If I am aware that I am dull, without comparison, that's quite different. How is it with you? Are you comparing yourself and therefore saying, "I am dull"? Or are you aware that you are dull, without

125

comparison? Can that be? Do please stay with that a little bit.

Questioner: Sir, is this possible?

Krishnamurti: Please give two minutes to this question. Am I aware that I am hungry because you tell me so, or do I feel hungry? If you tell me that I am hungry, I may feel a little hunger but it is not real hunger. But if I am hungry, I *am* hungry. So I must be very clear whether my dullness is the result of comparison. Then I can proceed from there.

Questioner: What has brought it home to you in such a way that you can leave it and only be concerned with whether you are dull or not?

Krishnamurti: Because I see the truth that comparison makes the mind dull. At school when one boy is compared with another boy, you destroy the boy comparing him with another. If you tell the younger brother that he must be as clever as the elder brother, you have destroyed the younger brother, haven't you? You are not concerned with the younger brother, you are concerned with the cleverness of the older boy.

Questioner: Can a dull mind look and find out if it is dull?

Krishnamurti: We are going to find out. Please let's begin again. Could we not stick to this one thing this morning?

Questioner: So long as there is that drive, what validity has it whether I am dull in myself or by comparison?

Krishnamurti: We are going to find out. Please, just go along with the speaker for a few minutes, not accepting or rejecting, but watching yourself. We said at the beginning of this morning's dialogue that the revolution must

126

take place at the very root of our being, and that it can take place only when we know how to observe what we are. The observation depends on the brightness, the clarity, and the openness of the mind that looks. But most of us are dull, and we say we see nothing when we look; we see anger, jealousy, and so on, but it doesn't result in anything. So we are concerned with the dull mind, not with what it is looking at. This dull mind says, "I must be clever in order to look." So it has a pattern of what cleverness is and is trying to become that. Somebody tells it, "Comparison will always produce dullness." So it says, "I must be terribly careful of that, I won't compare. I only knew what dullness was through comparison. If I don't compare, how do I know I am dull?" So I say to myself, "I won't call it dull." I won't use the word "dull" at all. I will only observe "what is" and not call it dull. Because the moment I call it dull, I have already given it a name and made it dull. But if I don't call it dull, but only observe, I have removed comparison, I have removed the word "dull" and there is only "what is." This is not difficult, is it? Please do watch it for yourself. Look what has happened now! Look where my mind is now.

Questioner: I see that my mind is too slow.

Krishnamurti: Will you please just listen. I'll go very slowly, step by step.

How do I realize my mind is dull? Because you have told me? Because I have read books that seem extraordinarily clever, intricate, and subtle? Or I have seen brilliant people and in comparing myself with them I call myself dull? I have to find out. So I won't compare; I refuse to compare myself with somebody else. Then do I know I am dull? Is the word preventing me to observe? Or is the word taking the place of "what actually is"? Are you following this? So I will not use a word, I won't call it dull, I won't call it slow, I won't call it anything, but find out "what is." So I have got rid of comparison, which is the most subtle thing. My mind has become extraordinarily intelligent because it doesn't compare, it doesn't use a word with which to see "what is," because it has realized the description is not the described. So what is actually the fact of "what is"?

Can we go from there? I am watching it, the mind is watching its own movement. Now do I condemn it, judge and evaluate and say, "This should be," "This should not be"? Has it any formula, any ideal, any resolution, any conclusion, which will inevitably distort "what is"? I have to go into that. If I have any conclusion I cannot look. If I am a moralist, if I am a respectable person, or a Christian, a Vedantist, or an "enlightened one," or this or that —all that prevents me from looking. Therefore I must be free of it all. I am watching if I have a conclusion of any kind. So the mind has become extraordinarily clear and it says, "Is there fear?" I watch it and I say, "There is fear, there is a desire for security, there is the urge for pleasure," and so on. I see that I cannot possibly look if there is any kind of conclusion, any kind of pleasurable movement taking place. So I am watching, and I find I am very traditional and I realize such a traditional mind can't look. My deep interest is to look and that deep interest shows me the danger of any conclusion. Therefore the very perception of danger is the discarding of that danger. So my mind then is not confused, it has no conclusion, does not think in terms of words, of descriptions, and is not comparing. Such a mind can observe and what it observes is itself. Therefore a revolution has taken place. Now you are lost—completely lost!

Questioner: I don't think that this revolution has taken place. Today I managed to look at the mind in the way you say, the mind becomes sharper, but tomorrow I will have forgotten how to look.

Krishnamurti: You can't forget it, Sir. Do you forget a snake? Do you forget a precipice? Do you forget the bottle

128

marked "poison"? You *can't* forget it. The gentleman asked, "How can I cleanse the instrument?" We said the cleansing of the instrument is to be aware how the instrument is made dull, clouded, unclear. We have described what makes it clouded, and we also said the description is not the actual thing described; so don't be caught in words. Be with the thing described, which is the instrument that is made dull.

Questioner: Surely if you look at yourself in the manner you described you expect something.

Krishnamurti: I am not expecting a transformation, enlightenment, a mutation, I am expecting nothing, because I don't know what is going to happen. I know only one thing very clearly, that the instrument that is looking is not clean, it is clouded, it is cracked. That's all I know and nothing else. And my only concern is, how can this instrument be made whole, healthy?

Questioner: Why are you looking?

Krishnamurti: The world is burning and the world is me. I am terribly disturbed, terribly confused, and there must be some order somewhere in all this. That is what is making me look. But if you say, "The world is all right, why do you bother about it, you have got good health and a little money, wife and children and a house, leave it alone"—then, of course, the world isn't burning. But it *is* burning all the same, whether you like it or not. So that is what makes me look, not some intellectual conception, nor some emotional excitement, but the actual fact that the world is burning—the wars, the hatred, the deception, the images, the false gods, and all the rest of it. And that very perception of what is taking place outwardly, makes me aware inwardly. And I say the inward state is the outward state, they are both one, indivisible.

Questioner: We are back at the very beginning. The fact is the dull mind doesn't see that by comparison it will think it should be different.

Krishnamurti: No, it is all wrong. I don't want to be different! I only see that the instrument is dull. I don't know what to do with it. So I am going to find out, which doesn't mean I want to change the instrument. I don't.

Questioner: Is using *any* word an obstacle to seeing?

Krishnamurti: The word is not the thing; therefore if you are looking at the thing, unless you put the word aside, it becomes extraordinarily important.

Questioner: I think that I disagree with you. When one looks, one sees the instrument has two parts, one is perception, the other is expression. It is impossible to sever these two parts. It is a linguistic problem, not one of dullness. The difficulty lies in language, in the randomness of expression.

Krishnamurti: Are you saying, in observation there is perception and expression, the two are not separate? Therefore when you perceive, there must also be the clarity of expression, the linguistic understanding, and the perception and the expression must never be separated, they must always go together. So you are saying that it is very important to use the right word.

Questioner: I am saying "expression," I am not saying "intention."

Krishnamurti: I understand—expression. Out of that comes another factor: perception, expression and action. If action is not expression and perception—expression being expressing it in words—then there is a fragmentation. So is not perception action? The very perceiving is the acting.

130

As when I perceive a precipice and there is immediate acting; that action is the expression of the perception. So perception and action can never be separated, therefore the ideal and action are impossible. If I see the stupidity of an ideal, the very perception of the stupidity of it is the action of intelligence. So the watching of dullness, the perceiving of dullness, is the clearing of the mind of dullness, which is action.

Saanen, Switzerland, August 6, 1969

11. The Art of Seeing

Awareness without time interval.
Tiger chasing tiger.

It is important, I think, to understand the nature and the beauty of observation, of seeing. As long as the mind is in any way distorted—by neurotic promptings and feelings, by fear, sorrow, by health, by ambition, snobbishness, and the pursuit of power—it cannot possibly listen, watch, see. The art of seeing, listening, watching, is not a thing to be cultivated, it is not a question of evolution and gradual growth. When one is aware of danger there is immediate action, the instinctual, instantaneous response of the body and memory. From childhood one has been conditioned that way to meet danger, so that the mind responds instantly, otherwise there is physical destruction. We are asking whether it is possible to act in the very *seeing* in which there is no conditioning at all. Can a mind respond freely and instantly to any form of distortion and therefore act? That is, perception, action, and expression are all one; they are not divided, broken up. The very seeing is the acting, which is the expression of that seeing. When there is an awareness of fear, observe it so intimately that the very observation of it is the freeing of it, which is action. Could we go into that this morning? I feel this is very important: we might be able to penetrate into the unknown. But a mind that is in any way deeply conditioned by its own fears, ambitions, greed, despair, and all the rest of it, cannot possibly penetrate into something that requires an extraordinarily healthy, sane, balanced, and harmonious being.

So our question is whether a mind—meaning the whole being—can be aware of a particular form of perversion, a particular form of striving, of violence, and seeing it can end it, not gradually but instantly. This means not allowing time to occur between perception and action. When you see danger there is no time interval, instant action takes place.

We are used to the idea that we will gradually become wise, enlightened, by watching, practicing, day after day. That is what we are used to, that is the pattern of our culture and our conditioning. Now we are saying this gradual process of the mind to free itself from fear or violence is to further fear and to encourage further violence.

Is it possible to end violence—not only outwardly but deep down at the very roots of our being—end the sense of aggression, the pursuit of power? In the very seeing of it completely, can we end it without allowing time to come into being? Can we discuss that this morning? Usually we allow time to enter the interval between seeing and acting, the lag between "what is" and "what should be." There is the desire to get rid of what is in order to achieve or to become something else. One must understand this time interval very clearly. We think in those terms because from childhood we are brought up and educated to think: eventually, gradually, we will be something. Outwardly, technologically one can see that time is necessary. I can't become a first-class carpenter, or physicist, or mathematician, without spending many years at it. One may have the clarity—I dislike to use the word "intuition"—to see a mathematical issue when one is quite young. And one realizes that to cultivate the memory that is demanded in learning a new technique or a new language, time is absolutely necessary. I can't speak German tomorrow, I need many months. I know nothing about electronics and to learn about it I need perhaps many years. So don't let's confuse the time element that is necessary in order to learn a technique with the danger of allowing time to interfere with perception and action.

Questioner: Should we talk about children, about growing up?

Krishnamurti: A child has to grow up. He has to learn so many things. When one says, "You must grow up," it is a rather derogatory word.

Questioner: Sir, partial psychological change does take place within us.

Krishnamurti: Of course! One has been angry, or one is angry, and one says "I musn't be angry" and gradually one works at it and brings about a partial state when one is a little less angry, less irritable and more controlled.

Questioner: I don't mean that.

Krishnamurti: Then what do you mean, Madam?

Questioner: I mean something that you have and you have dropped. There may be confusion again, but it's not the same.

Krishnamurti: Yes, but is it not always the same confusion, only a little modified? There is a modified continuity. You may stop depending on somebody, going through the pain of dependence and the ache of loneliness, and saying, "I will no longer be dependent." And perhaps you will be able to drop it. So you say a certain change has taken place. The next dependence will not be exactly the same as it was before. And again you go into it and you drop it and so on. Now we are asking whether it is possible to see the whole nature of dependence and instantly be free of it—not gradually—as you would act immediately when there is danger. This is really an important issue into which

134

we should go not only verbally but deeply, inwardly. Watch the implication of it. The whole of Asia believes in reincarnation: that is, one will be born again in the next life depending on how you have lived in this life. If you have lived brutally, aggressively, destructively, you are going to pay for it in the next life. You don't necessarily become an animal, you go back to a human state living a more painful, more destructive life, because before you have not lived a life of beauty. Those who believe in this idea of reincarnation, believe only in the word, but not in the depth of the meaning of that word. What you do *now* matters infinitely for tomorrow—because tomorrow, which is the next life, you are going to pay for it. So the idea of gradually attaining different forms is essentially the same in the East and in the West. There is always this time element, the "what is" and "what should be." To achieve what should be requires time, time being effort, concentration, attention. As one has not got attention or concentration, there is a constant effort to practice attention, which requires time.

There must be a different way altogether of tackling this problem. One must understand perception, both seeing and action; they are not separate, they are not divided. We must equally inquire into the question of action, of doing. What is action, the doing?

Questioner: How can a blind man who has no perception, act?

Krishnamurti: Have you ever tried putting a band round your eyes for a week? We did, for fun. You know, you develop other sensitivities, your senses become much sharper. Before you come to the wall or the chair or the desk, you already know it is there. We are talking of being blind to ourselves, inwardly. We are terribly aware of things outwardly, but inwardly we are blind.

What is action? Is action always based on an idea, a principle, a belief, a conclusion, a hope, a despair? If one

135

has an idea, an ideal, one is conforming to that ideal; there is an interval between the ideal and the act. That interval is time. "I shall be that ideal"—by identifying myself with that ideal, eventually that ideal will act and there will be no separation between action and the ideal. What takes place when there is this ideal and the action that is approximating itself to the ideal? In that time interval what takes place?

Questioner: Incessant comparison.

Krishnamurti: Yes, comparison and all the rest of it. What action takes place, if you observe?

Questioner: We ignore the present.

Krishnamurti: Then, what else?

Questioner: Contradiction.

Krishnamurti: It is a contradiction. It leads to hypocrisy. I am angry and the ideal says, "Don't be angry." I am suppressing, controlling, conforming, approximating myself to the ideal and therefore I am always in conflict and pretending. The idealist is a person who pretends. Also, in this division there is conflict. There are other factors which come into being.

Questioner: Why aren't we allowed to remember our former lives? Our evolution would be much easier.

Krishnamurti: Would it?

Questioner: We could avoid mistakes.

Krishnamurti: What do you mean by former life? The life of yesterday, twenty-four hours ago?

Questioner: The last incarnation.

Krishnamurti: Which is a hundred years ago? How would it make life easier?

Questioner: We would understand better.

Krishnamurti: Please follow it step by step—you would have the memory of what you did or did not do, of what you suffered a hundred years ago, which is exactly the same as yesterday. Yesterday you did many things which you like or regret, which caused you pain, despair and sorrow. There is the memory of all that. And you have the memory of a thousand years, which is essentially the same as yesterday. Why call *that* reincarnation, and not the incarnation of yesterday, which is being born today? You see, we don't like that because we think we are extraordinary beings, or we have time to grow, to become, to reincarnate. What it is that reincarnates you have never looked at—which is your memory. There is nothing sacred or holy about it. Your memory of yesterday is being born today in what you are doing; the yesterday is controlling what you are doing today. And a thousand years of memories are operating through yesterday and through today. So there is constant incarnation of the past. Don't think this is a clever way out of it, an explanation. When one sees the importance of memory and the utter futility of it, then one will never talk about reincarnation.

We are asking what action is. Is action ever free, spontaneous, immediate? Or is action always bound by time, which is thought, which is memory?

Questioner: I was watching a cat catching a mouse. She doesn't think, "It's a mouse"; immediately, instinctively, she catches it. It seems to me we must also act spontaneously.

Krishnamurti: Not "we must," "we should." Sir, please
—I think we shall never say "we should," "we must,"
when we understand the time element essentially. We
are asking ourselves, not verbally, not intellectually, but
deeply, inwardly, what is action? Is action always time
binding? Action born out of a memory, out of fear, out
of despair, is always time binding. Is there an action
which is completely free and therefore free of time?

Questioner: You say one sees a snake and acts immediately. But snakes grow with action. Life is not so simple,
there is not only one snake, but two snakes, and it becomes like a mathematical problem. Then time comes in.

Krishnamurti: You are saying we live in a world of tigers
and one doesn't meet only one tiger but a dozen tigers in
human form, who are brutal, violent, avaricious, greedy,
each one pursuing his own particular delight. And to
live and to act in that world you need time to kill one
tiger after another. The tiger is myself—is in me—there
are a dozen tigers in me. And you said, to get rid of those
tigers, one by one, you need time. That is just what we are
questioning altogether. We have accepted that it requires
time to gradually kill those snakes which are in me one
after the other. The "me" is the "you"— the "you" with
your tigers, with your serpents—all this is also the "me."
And we say, why kill those animals which are in me one
after the other? There are a thousand "me's" inside me, a
thousand snakes, and by the time I have killed them all I
shall be dead.

So is there a way—do please listen to it, don't answer
it, find out—of getting rid of all the snakes at once, not
gradually? Can I see the danger of all the animals, all the
contradictions in me and be free of them instantly? If I
cannot do it, then there is no hope for me. I can pretend
all kinds of things but if I cannot wipe away everything
that is in me immediately, I am a slave forever, whether
I am reborn in a next life or in ten thousand lives. So I

have to find a way of acting, of looking, that brings to an
end in the instant of perception, brings to an end the
particular dragon, the particular monkey in me.

Questioner: Do it!

Krishnamurti: No, Madam, please, this is really an extraordinary question, you can't just say "do this" or "don't do
that." This requires a tremendous inquiry; don't tell me
that you have got it or that you should do this or that,
that doesn't interest me—I want to find out.

Questioner: If only I could see it!

Krishnamurti: No, please, not "if."

Questioner: If I perceive something, should I put it into
words or just let it remain in me?

Krishnamurti: Why do you translate what has been said
in very simple language into your own words—why can't
you see what is being said? We have got many animals
in us, many dangers. Can I be free of them all with *one*
perception—seeing immediately? You may have done it,
Madam, I am not questioning whether you have done it
or not, that would be impudence on my part. But I am
asking, is this possible?

Questioner: Action has two parts. The inner, decisional
part takes place immediately. The action toward the outer
world needs time. Decision means inner action. To bridge
over these two aspects of action necessitates time. This is
a problem of language, of transmission.

Krishnamurti: I understand, Sir. There is outward action
which needs time, and inward action which is perception
and action. How is this inward action, with its perception,
decision and immediate action, to be bridged over to the
other action which needs time? Is the question clear?

If I may point out, I do not think it requires a bridge. There is no bridging over or connecting the two. I'll show you what I mean. I realize very clearly that to go from here to there takes time, to learn a language needs time, to do anything physically needs time. Is time necessary inwardly? If I can understand the nature of time, then I will deal with the time element in the outer world rightly, and not let that interfere with the inward state. So I am not beginning with the outer, because I recognize the outer needs time. But I am asking myself whether in inward perception, decision, action, time is there at all. Therefore I am asking, "Is decision necessary at all?"—decision being an instant part of time—a second, a point. "I decide" means there *is* an element of time; decision is based on will and desire, all that implies time. So I am asking, why should decision enter into this at all? Or is that decision part of my conditioning which says, "You must have time."

So is there perception and action without decision? That is, I am aware of fear, a fear brought about by thought, by past memories, by experiences, the incarnation of that yesterday's fear into today. I have understood the whole nature, the structure, the inwardness of fear. And the seeing of it without decision is action which is the freedom from it. Is this possible? Don't say yes, I have done it, or somebody else has done it—that's not the point. Can this fear end instantly on its arising? There are the superficial fears, which are the fears of the world. The world is full of tigers and those tigers, which are part of me, are going to destroy; therefore there is a war between me—a part of the tiger—and the rest of the tigers.

There is also inward fear—being psychologically insecure, psychologically uncertain—all brought about by thought. Thought breeds pleasure, thought breeds fear— I see all that. I see the danger of fear as I see the danger of a snake, of a precipice, of deep running water—I see the danger completely. And the very seeing is the ending, without the interval of even the slightest second of making a decision.

Questioner: Sometimes you can recognize a fear and yet you still have that fear.

Krishnamurti: One has to go into this very carefully. First of all, I don't want to get rid of fear. I want to express it, to understand it, to let it flow, let it come, explode in me, and all the rest of it. I don't know anything about fear. I know I am afraid. Now I want to find out what level, at what depth I am afraid, consciously, or at the very root, at the deep levels of my being—in the caves, in the unexplored regions of my mind. I want to find out. I want it all to come out, be exposed. So how shall I do that? I must do it —not gradually—you understand? It must come out of my being completely.

Questioner: If there are a thousand tigers and I sit on the ground I can't see them. But if I move to a plain above I can deal with them.

Krishnamurti: Not "if." "If I could fly I would see the beauty of the earth." I can't fly, I am here. I am afraid those theoretical questions have no value at all and apparently we don't realize that. I am hungry and you are feeding me with theories. Here is a problem, do please look at it, because we are all afraid, everyone has fear of some kind or another. There are deep, hidden fears and I am very well aware of the superficial fears, the fears of the world; the fears that arise out of losing a job or of this and that—losing my wife, my son. I know that very well. Perhaps there are deeper layers of fears. How am I, how is this mind to expose all that instantly? What do you say?

Questioner: Do you say that we must chase the animal away once and for all or do we have to hunt it every time?

Krishnamurti: The questioner says, you are suggesting that it is possible to chase the animal away entirely, forever, not chase it one day and let it come back the next day. That is

141

what we are saying. I don't want to chase the animal repeatedly. That is what all the schools, all the saints and all the religions and psychologists say: chase it away little by little. It doesn't mean a thing to me. I want to find out how to chase the animal away so that it will never come back. And when it comes back I know what to do, I won't let it enter the house. You understand?

Questioner: We must now give the animal its right name: it is thought. And when it comes back we'll know what to do with it.

Krishnamurti: I don't know what to do—we'll see. You are all so eager!

Questioner: This is our life—we have to be eager!

Krishnamurti: Eager to answer (was meant). Of course we have to be eager. This is such a difficult subject; you can't just throw in a lot of words. This requires care.

Questioner: Why don't we actually do perception right now?

Krishnamurti: That is what I am proposing.

Questioner: What happens if I look at you? First I get a presentation of you. Please look at me. The first thing that happens is the visual presentation of me, right? Then what happens? Thought happens about the presentation.

Krishnamurti: That's what the lady was saying, exactly the same thing. Thought is the animal. Stick to that animal, please. Don't say the animal is thought, or the self, the me, the ego, fear, greed, envy, and then go back to another description of it. That animal, we say, is *all* this. And we see that animal cannot be chased out gradually, because it will always come back in different forms. Being somewhat aware, I say: how stupid all this is, this constant chasing of the animal—its coming back and chasing it again. I want to find out if it is possible to chase it completely away so that it will never come back.

Questioner: I see different functions in myself, with different velocities. If one function pursues another, nothing happens. For instance, if emotion pursues idea. One must look with all functions.

Krishnamurti: It is the same thing you are putting into different words.

Questioner: You started to give an explanation which was interrupted. You began to say that you did not want to get rid of fear at all.

Krishnamurti: I said to you, first of all, I don't want to get rid of the animal. I don't want to chase him out. Before I take the whip or the velvet glove, I want to know who is chasing him out. Perhaps it may be a bigger tiger that is chasing him out. So I say to myself, I don't want to chase anything out. See the importance of it!

Questioner: Chasing out might be your eventual death sentence.

Krishnamurti: No, I don't know. Go slow, Sir, let me explain. I say before I chase the animal, I want to find out who is the entity that is going to chase it. And I say, it may be a bigger tiger. If I want to get rid of all the tigers, it is no good getting a bigger tiger to chase the little tiger. So I say wait, I don't want to chase anything out. See what is happening to my mind. I don't want to chase anything out but I want to look. I want to observe, I want to be very clear whether a bigger tiger is chasing a little tiger. This game will go on forever, that's what is going on in the world—the tyranny of one particular country chasing a smaller country.

So I am now very aware—please follow this—that I mustn't chase *anything*. I must root out this principle of chasing something out, overcoming it, dominating it. Because the decision which says "I must get rid of that tiny little tiger" may grow into the big tiger. So there must be complete cessation of all decision, of all the urge to get rid of something, to chase away anything. Then I can look. Then I say to myself (I mean this verbally), "I won't chase anything away." Therefore I am free of the burden of time, which is to chase one tiger with another tiger. In that there is a time interval and so I say, "Therefore I won't do a thing, I won't chase, I won't act, I won't decide, I must first look."

I am looking—I don't mean the ego, but the mind is looking, the brain is watching. I can spot the various tigers, the mother tiger with her cubs and the husband; I can watch all that but there must be deeper things inside me and I want them all exposed. Shall I expose them through action, through doing? Getting more and more angry and then calming down, and a week later again getting angry and then calming down? Or is there a way of looking at all the tigers, the little one, the big one, the one just being born —all of them? Can I watch them all so completely that I've understood the whole business? If I am not capable of that, then my life will go on in the old routine, in the bourgeois way, the complicated, the stupid, the cunning way. That's all. So if you have known how to listen the morning's sermon is over.

Do you remember the story of a master speaking to his disciples every morning? One day he gets onto the rostrum and a little bird comes and sits on the windowsill and begins to sing and the master lets it sing. After it has been singing for a while it flies away. And the master says to the disciples, "This morning's sermon is over."

Saanen, Switzerland, August 7, 1969

12. On Penetrating into the Unknown

**Suppression. Action out of stillness.
Voyage into oneself. False journeys
and the projected "unknown."**

We were asking how to put aside the whole menagerie
that one has in oneself. We are discussing all this because
we see—at least I see—that one has to penetrate into the
unknown. After all, any good mathematician or physicist
must investigate the unknown and perhaps also the artist,
if he is not too carried away by his own emotions and
imagination. And we, the ordinary people with everyday
problems, also have to live with a deep sense of understanding. We too have to penetrate into the unknown. A
mind that is always chasing the animals that it has invented, the dragons, the serpents, the monkeys, with all
their troubles and their contradictions—which we are—
cannot possibly penetrate into the unknown. Being just
ordinary people, not endowed with brilliant intellects or
great visions, but just living daily, monotonous, ugly little
lives, we are concerned how to change all that immediately.
That is what we are considering.

People change with new inventions, new pressures, new
theories, new political situations; all those bring about a
certain quality of change. But we are talking about a
radical, basic revolution in one's being and whether such
a revolution is to be brought about gradually or instantly.
Yesterday we went into all that is involved in bringing it
about gradually, the whole sense of distance and the time
and effort needed to reach that distance. And we said,

man has tried this for millennia, but somehow he has not been able to change radically—except perhaps for one or two. So it is necessary to see whether we can, each one of us and therefore the world—because the world is us and we are the world, they are not two separate states—instantly wipe away all the travail, the anger, the hatred, the enmity that we have created and the bitterness that one bears. Apparently bitterness is one of the commonest things to have; can that bitterness, knowing all its causes, seeing its whole structure, be wiped away on the instant?

We said that is possible only when there is observation. When the mind can observe very intensely, then that very observation is the action which ends bitterness. We also went into the question of what is action: whether there is any free, spontaneous, nonvolitional action. Or is action based on our memory, on our ideals, on our contradictions, on our hurts, our bitterness and so on? Is action always approximating itself to an ideal, to a principle, to a pattern? And we said, such action is not action at all, because it creates contradiction between what "should be" and "what is." When you have an ideal there is the distance to be covered between what you are and what you should be. That "should be" may take years, or as many believe, many lives incarnating over and over again till you reach that perfect Utopia. We also said there is the incarnation of yesterday into today; whether that yesterday stretches back many millennia or only twenty-four hours, it is still operating when there is action based on this division between the past, the present and the future, which is "what should be." All this, we said, brings about contradiction, conflict, misery; it is not action. Perceiving is action; the very perception *is* action, which takes place when you are confronted with a danger; then there is instant action. I think we came to that point yesterday.

There is also the instant when there is a great crisis, a challenge, or a great sorrow. Then the mind is for an instant extraordinarily quiet, it is shocked. I don't know if you have observed it. When you see the mountain in the evening or in the early morning, with that extraordinary light on it, the shadows, the immensity, the majesty, the feeling of deep aloneness—when you see all that your mind cannot take it all in; for the moment it is completely quiet. But it soon overcomes that shock and responds according to its own conditioning, its own particular personal problems and so on. So there is an instant when the mind is completely quiet, but it cannot sustain that sense of absolute stillness. That stillness can be produced by a shock. Most of us know this sense of absolute stillness when there is a great shock. Either it can be produced outwardly by some incident, or it can be brought about artificially, inwardly, by a series of impossible questions as in some Zen school, or by some imaginative state, some formula which forces the mind to be quiet—which is obviously rather childish and immature. We are saying that for a mind that is capable of perception in the sense we have been talking about, that very perception is action. To perceive, the mind must be completely still, otherwise it can't see. If I want to listen to what you are saying, I must listen silently. Any vagrant thought, any interpretation of what you are saying, any sense of resistance prevents the actual listening.

So the mind that wants to listen, observe, see or watch must of necessity be extraordinarily quiet. That quietness cannot possibly be brought about through any sense of shock or through absorption in a particular idea. When a child is absorbed in a toy it is very quiet, it is playing. But the toy has absorbed the mind of the child, the toy has made the child quiet. In taking a drug or in doing anything artificial, there is this sense of being absorbed by something greater—a picture, an image, a Utopia. This still, quiet mind can come about only through the understanding of all the contradictions, perversions, conditioning, fears, distortions. We are asking whether those fears, miseries, confusions, can all be wiped away instantly, so that the mind is quiet to observe, to penetrate.

Can one actually do it? Can you actually look at yourself with complete quietness? When the mind is active then it is distorting what it sees, translating, interpreting, saying "I like this," "I don't like it." It gets tremendously excited and emotional and such a mind cannot possibly see.

So we are asking, can ordinary human beings like us do this? Can I look at myself, whatever I am, knowing the danger of words like "fear" or "bitterness" and that the very word is going to prevent the actual seeing of "what is"? Can I observe, being aware of the pitfalls of language? Also, not allowing any sense of time to interfere—any sense of "to achieve," "to get rid of"—but just observe, quietly, intently, attentively. In that state of intense attention, the hidden paths, the undiscovered recesses of the mind are seen. In that there is no analysis whatsoever, only perception. Analysis implies time and also the analyzer and the analyzed. Is the analyzer different from the thing analyzed?—if it is not, there is no sense in analysis. One has to be aware of all this, discard it all—time, analysis, resistance, trying to reach across, overcome and so on—because through that door there is no end to sorrow.

After listening to all this, can one actually do it? This is really an important question. There is no "how." There is nobody to tell you what to do and give you the necessary energy. It requires great energy to observe: a still mind is the total energy without any wastage, otherwise it is not still. And can one look at oneself with this total energy so completely that the seeing is acting and therefore the ending?

Questioner: Sir, is not your question equally impossible?

Krishnamurti: Is this an impossible question? If it is an impossible question then why are you all sitting here? Just to listen to the voice of a man talking, to listen to the stream going by, have a nice holiday among these hills and mountains and meadows? Why can't you do it? Is it so difficult? Is it a matter of having a very clever brain? Or is it that you have never in your life actually observed yourself and therefore you find this so impossible? One has to do something when the house is burning! You don't say, "It is impossible, I don't believe it, I can't do anything about it," and sit and watch it burn! You do something in relation to the actuality, not something in relation to what you think should be. The actuality is the house burning—you may not be able to put the fire out completely before the fire engine comes, but in the meantime—there is no "in the meantime" at all—you act in relation to the fire.

So when you say it's an impossible question, as difficult, as impossible as putting a duck into a little bottle—it shows that you are not aware that the house is burning. Why isn't one aware that the house is burning? The house means the world, the world which is you, with your discontent, with all the things that are going on inside you and the world outside you. If you are not aware of this, why aren't you? Is it that one is not clever, that one has not read innumerable books, is not sensitive to know what is happening inside oneself and not aware of what is actually going on? If you say, "Sorry, I'm not," then why aren't you? You are aware when you are hungry, when somebody insults you. You are very much aware if someone flatters you or when you want fulfillment of sexual desires; then you are very much aware. But here you say, "I am not." So what is one to do? Rely on somebody's stimulation and encouragement?

Questioner: You say that there has to be a mutation and that this can be done by watching one's thoughts and desires and this has to be done instantly. I have once done this and there has been no change. If we do what you suggest, is it then a permanent state, or must it be done regularly, daily?

Krishnamurti: This perception which is action, can this be done once and for all, or must it be done every day? What do you think?

149

Questioner: I think it can be done after listening to music.

Krishnamurti: Therefore music becomes necessary like a drug, only music is much more respectable than a drug. The question is this: must one watch every day, every minute, or can one watch it so completely one day that the whole thing ends? Can I go to sleep for the rest of the time, once I've seen the thing completely? You understand the question? I am afraid one has to watch every day and not go to sleep. You have to be aware, not only of insults, of flattery, of anger, of despair, but also of all the things that are happening around you and inside you all the time. You can't say, "Now I'm completely enlightened, nothing will touch me."

Questioner: At the moment, or the minute, or the time that it takes to get this perception and to understand what has happened, are you not then suppressing a violent reaction you had when the insult came? Isn't this perception simply the suppression of the reaction which would take place? Instead of reacting you perceive instead—the perception may just be the suppression of the reaction.

Krishnamurti: We went into this pretty thoroughly, didn't we? I have a reaction of dislike—I don't like you and I watch that reaction. If I watch it very attentively it unfolds, it exposes my conditioning, the culture in which I have been brought up. If I am still watching and have not gone to sleep, if the mind is watching what has been exposed, many, many things are revealed—there is no question of suppression at all. Because I am interested to see what is happening, not in how to go beyond all the reactions. I am interested to find out whether the mind can look, perceive the very structure of the me, the ego, the self. And in that, how can any form of suppression exist?

Questioner: I sometimes feel a state of stillness; can there be action out of that stillness?

Krishnamurti: Are you asking, "How can this stillness be maintained, sustained, kept going?"—is that it?

Questioner: Can I go on with my daily work?

Krishnamurti: Can the daily activities come out of silence? You are all waiting for me to answer this. I have a horror of being an oracle; because I happen to be sitting on a platform it doesn't give me any authority. This is the question: can the mind that is very still act in daily life? If you separate the daily life from stillness, from the Utopia, from the ideal—which is silence—then the two will never meet. Can I keep the two divided, can I say this is the world, my daily life, and this is the silence which I have experienced, which I have felt my way into? Can I translate that silence into daily life? You can't. But if the two are not separate—the right hand is the left hand—and there is harmony between the two, between silence and the daily life, when there is unity, then one will never ask, "Can I act out of silence?"

Questioner: You are talking of intense awareness, intense looking, intense seeing. Could it not be said that the degree of intensity that one has is primarily what makes it possible?

Krishnamurti: One is essentially intense and there is that deep, basic intensity which one has—is that it?

Questioner: The way one comes to it with a passion, not for *its* sake, but it seems to be a primary requirement.

Krishnamurti: Which we have already. Yes?

Questioner: Yes and no.

Krishnamurti: Sir, why do we assume so many things? Can one not take a voyage and examine, not knowing anything?

151

A voyage into oneself, not knowing what is good or bad, what is right or wrong, what should be, what must be, but just take the voyage without any burden? That is one of the most difficult things, to voyage inwardly without any sense of burden. And as you voyage you discover—you don't start and say at the beginning, "This must not be so," "This should be." Apparently that is one of the most difficult things to do, I don't know why. Look, Sirs, there is nobody to help, including the speaker. There is nobody in whom to have faith, and I hope you have no faith in *anybody*. There is no authority to tell you what is or what should be, to walk in one direction, not in another, to mind the pitfalls, all marked out for you—you are walking alone. Can you do that? You say, "I can't do it because I am afraid." Then take fear and go into it and understand it completely. Forget about the journey, forget about authority—examine this whole thing called fear—fear, because you have nobody to lean on, nobody to tell you what to do, fear because you might make a mistake. Make a mistake, and in observing the mistake you will jump out of it instantly.

Discover as you go along. In this there is greater creativeness than in painting, writing a book, going on the stage and making a monkey of oneself. There is greater—if I can use the word—excitement, a greater sense of—

Questioner: Exaltation?

Krishnamurti: Oh, don't supply the word.

Questioner: If daily life is performed without introducing an observer, then nothing disturbs the silence.

Krishnamurti: That is the whole problem. But the observer is always playing tricks, is always casting a shadow and thereby bringing further problems. We are asking whether you and I can take a journey inwardly, not knowing a thing and discovering as we go along, one's sexual appetites, one's

152

cravings, intentions. It is a tremendous adventure, much greater than going to the moon.

Questioner: This is the problem; they knew where they were going, they knew the direction when they undertook to go to the moon. Inwardly there is no direction.

Krishnamurti: The gentleman says, going to the moon is objective, we know where to go. Here, taking a journey inwardly, we don't know where we are going. Therefore there is insecurity and fear. If you know where you are going you will never penetrate into the unknown; and therefore you will never be the real person who discovers what is the eternal.

Questioner: Can there be total, immediate perception without the help of a master?

Krishnamurti: That's what we've been talking about.

Questioner: We didn't finish the other question; this is a problem because we know where we are going; we want to hold on to pleasure, we don't really want the unknown.

Krishnamurti: Yes, we want to hold on to the apronstrings of pleasure. We want to hold on to the things that we know. And with all that we want to take a journey. Have you ever climbed a mountain? The more you are burdened the more difficult it is. Even to go up these little hills is quite difficult if you carry a burden. And if you climb a mountain you have to be much freer. I really don't know what the difficulty is. We want to carry with us everything we know— the insults, the resistances, the stupidities, the delights, the exaltations, everything that we have had. When you say, "I'm going to take a journey carrying all that," you are taking a journey somewhere else, not into that which you are carrying. Therefore your journey is in imagination, is unreality. But take a journey into the things which you are carrying, the known—not into the unknown—into what you already know: your pleasures, your delights, your despairs, your sorrows. Take a journey into that, that is all you have. You say, "I want to take a journey with all that into the unknown and add the unknown to it, add other delights, other pleasures." Or it may be so dangerous that you say, "I don't want to."

Saanen, Switzerland, August 8, 1969